THE PERSISTENCE OF FAITH

THE REITH LECTURES 1990

THE PERSISTENCE
OF FAITH

Religion, Morality and Society
in a Secular Age

JONATHAN SACKS

BLOOMSBURY CONTINUUM
LONDON · OXFORD · NEW YORK · NEW DELHI · SYDNEY

BLOOMSBURY CONTINUUM
Bloomsbury Publishing Plc
50 Bedford Square, London, WC1B 3DP, UK
Bloomsbury Publishing Ireland Limited,
29 Earlsfort Terrace, Dublin 2, D02 AY28, Ireland

BLOOMSBURY, BLOOMSBURY CONTINUUM and the Diana logo are
trademarks of Bloomsbury Publishing Plc

First published by Weidenfeld Paperbacks in 1991
Reprinted by Bloomsbury Continuum 2005
This edition published 2025

A catalogue record for this book is available from the British Library

Library of Congress Cataloguing-in-Publication data has been applied for

ISBN: PB: 978-1-3994-2079-2; eBook: 978-1-3994-2078-5;
ePDF: 978-1-3994-2075-4

2 4 6 8 10 9 7 5 3 1

Typeset by Deanta Global Publishing Services, Chennai, India
Printed and bound in Great Britain by Clays Ltd, Elcograf S.p.A.

To find out more about our authors and books visit www.bloomsbury.com
and sign up for our newsletters

For product safety related questions contact productsafety@bloomsbury.com

For
LOUISE PURSLOW

CONTENTS

PREFACE

The concerns I voiced in 1990, in the Reith Lectures reprinted here still exist. Already then I sensed that, in a secular Britain, we were misreading the signs. Religion was neither dead nor dying as a force in the world. Secularisation was neither complete nor irreversible. The reaction against it would take the form not of mild religiosity but of fundamentalism. There was a danger that multiculturalism was creating a 'society of conflicting ghettoes'. We were not about to witness the 'end of history', the bloodless worldwide triumph of democratic capitalism. Given all that has happened since 11 September 2001, these warnings turned out to be far milder than they should have been.

Much has happened since 1990 that could not have been predicted then: the Internet, the decoding of the human genome, the accelerating pace of globalisation, ethnic conflict in the Balkans and many other parts of the world, the savage massacre in Rwanda, and the rise and fall of the peace process in the Middle East. Worst has been the spread of terror as a tactical weapon against the West. A new kind of violence has entered our world – not classic terror aimed at strategic targets but terror as symbolic gesture in a religiously-defined cosmic struggle. To say that we have not yet understood what this represents and how it is to be confronted would be the understatement of the age.

Looking back on what I wrote fifteen years ago, there are three arguments I would re-emphasise. The first is the hard work we must undertake to give multicultural societies a sense of shared identity. The Jews who came to Britain as refugees, among them my late father, became passionately British as well as Jewish. They saw no contradiction between the two; nor should we. In the secular state there is no incompatibility between religious and national identities. None the less, a sense of collective belonging does not happen without sustained and focused effort. I argued then, and believe still, that each of us has to learn to be 'bilingual', at home in two identities, one we share with fellow believers, the other we share with fellow citizens. The second has become all the more important given the power of globalisation to undermine national identities. If Britain, or England, is where we happen to be, not where we belong, the danger of a nationalist backlash will grow.

The second relates to what I called in the second lecture 'demoralisation'. The waning of a moral consensus in the West, once predicated on religious belief, has left us dangerously ill-equipped to deal with some of the most fateful dilemmas ever confronted by mankind, from genetic intervention to ecological destruction from growing economic inequalities within and between societies, to the vexed question of international intervention in defence of human rights. It is not that we will have nothing to say about these issues. It is that we will lack the shared vocabulary necessary for civil discourse and reasoned public debate. Already, the power of the media is greater than that of most parliaments, and the media are constructed to favour an adversarial rather than consensual approach to conflict. It is not only terrorists but a whole range of single issue activists who have learned that direct action gets you more publicity than rational persuasion and the democratic process.

Thirdly, I remain convinced that, in many conflict zones throughout the world, if religion does not become part of the solution, it will be part of the problem. We have not yet learned what it is for religion to be a force for peace in our hyper-connected age. That will take courage, imagination and generosity of spirit, but as the famous rabbi of pre-Christian times, Hillel, said: If not now, when? There is no doubt that religions today face their greatest challenge since the wars of religion that changed the face of Europe in the sixteenth and seventeenth centuries. Faith persists. So does religious conflict. In the short term, wars are won by weapons; in the long run, by ideas. We need new ideas about what it means to honour human difference while at the same time renewing the global covenant of mankind.

Jonathan Sacks
November 2004

INTRODUCTION

In the course of his observations about the newly emerging *Democracy in America*, Alexis de Tocqueville remarked: 'Eighteenth century philosophers had a very simple explanation for the gradual weakening of beliefs. Religious zeal, they said, was bound to die down as enlightenment and freedom spread. It is tiresome that the facts do not fit this theory at all.'[1] Those sentences were written in the 1830s, but they are still germane in the 1990s and they frame the argument of *The Persistence of Faith*.

In recent decades, religion has taken us unawares. The rise of the Moral Majority in America in the 1970s, the Islamic revolution in Iran in 1979, the growth of religious parties in Israel, the power of Catholicism in Poland, the strength of reaction to Salman Rushdie's *The Satanic Verses*: all of these were unexpected developments that ran wholly contrary to the thesis that modernity and secularisation went hand-in-hand and could almost be regarded as synonyms. Instead and against all prediction, religion has resurfaced in the public domain.

This is not to say that an orthodox religious believer would necessarily welcome all these developments as such. Many of them could be categorised by the term 'fundamentalism', and if that signifies the attempt to impose a single religious vision on a society by political means, then I believe it runs counter to the religious imperative of a highly plural world. John Plamenatz once wrote that 'Liberty of conscience was born, not of indifference, not of scepticism, not of mere open-mindedness, but of faith,'[2] and with that sentiment I profoundly agree.

1

Religious extremism in the modern world is not simply the restoration of faith in its traditional form, but the aggressive reassertion of faith in an anti-traditional age. Nonetheless, its appearance in the major world religions in the past twenty years suggests that our predictions need to be revised.

The model that governed these predictions was *secularisation*. Matthew Arnold gave it its most memorable image when he wrote in his poem *Dover Beach* of the 'melancholy, long, withdrawing roar' of the retreating 'Sea of Faith'. Sociologists put it more prosaically. Bryan Wilson described it as 'the process in which religious consciousness, activities and institutions lose social significance.'[3] Peter Berger defined it as 'the process by which sectors of society and culture are removed from the domination of religious institutions and symbols.'[4] These are more than different ways of saying the same thing. Secularisation is a complex process occurring across several dimensions. It has proved hard to define and harder still to measure. But the drift of the argument was clear. Religion was losing its sovereignty over most areas of society. In advanced technological capitalisms it might not disappear altogether, but it would have lost its potency. It would be progressively relegated to the margins of private life.

How could it be otherwise? Modernity was a one-way street and religion had been caught facing in the wrong direction. Science had displaced it as a source of knowledge. Liberalism had dethroned it from the seat of political power. Post-enlightenment ethics had shattered its moral base of authority and obedience. Social changes had destroyed the communities in which it grew. If religious faith survived at all, it would be in the form of private consolation. As Bryan Wilson put it, 'It offers another world to explore as an escape from the rigors of technological order and the ennui that is the incidental by-product of an increasingly programmed world.'[5]

This was cold comfort. It placed religion on the level of the latest science fiction film fantasy: a temporary retreat from reality into illusion. Nor was Wilson alone. The image of religion as illusion has dominated the modern mind since Marx, Feuerbach and Freud. To see it as such is already to have embarked on the process that Max Weber called 'disenchantment', the gradual displacement of the supernatural. Politics, the economy, education, morality, the family, leisure and the arts had severally declared their independence from religion, which was left as the secret solace of the soul. Religion was neither the engine that drove society nor the map that directed its driver. It was at most a tape played on a mental stereo to while away the idle hours.

My experience of the contemporary Jewish world, as well as my readings of parallel developments in Christianity and Islam, convinced me that this was not what was happening, at least not in the last few decades. It was not that secularisation had not occurred: manifestly it has. It is, rather, that it has been accompanied by unexpected accommodations, resistances and counter-currents. There have been new religious forms and reforms, and an unanticipated resurgence of conservative religious movements. The Sea of Faith has neither retreated nor has there been a turn of the tide. Rather, there have been turbulences: unsettling shifts in all directions. De Tocqueville was right. The facts do not fit the theory at all.

THE CASE OF JUDAISM

Consider the case of Judaism. Modernity struck European Jewry with shattering force in the form of civil emancipation. Hitherto Jews had been excluded from the mainstream of European society. That fact, whatever its cost in terms of powerlessness, had at least served to reinforce Jewish identity. Jews were, and were conscious of being, a people apart.

They had their own structures of law and self-government. Religiously, culturally and linguistically, they formed a distinctive community. External circumstance matched internal self-definition. Jews, scattered and dispersed, saw themselves as a nation in exile, heirs to a covenant that had predicted their wanderings and foretold a future return to their land. Their persecutions and expulsions, their strange isolation, all served to confirm their religious self-understanding.

Emancipation changed that fundamentally. The terms of the transformation were set out in 1789, in the wake of the French Revolution. In the debate of the French National Assembly on the eligibility of Jews for citizenship in the new republic, Jews were invited to become citizens of the secular state, but at the price of ceasing to regard themselves as a separate community. No longer were they to be members of the Jewish nation in exile. Instead they were to be French citizens of the Jewish persuasion. The cost of emancipation was that Jews would have to undergo that most characteristic change of modernity: the *privatisation of faith*.

Previously, Jewish identity had been a total one, a matter of dress and speech, manners and mannerisms as much of prayer and precept: in short, a complete culture woven out of a religious cloth. Now it was to become a mere segment of a more complex totality. Jews would speak, dress and act like Frenchmen, and would be Jews primarily in the synagogue and home. Jewishness was no longer a taken-for-granted reality, an environment. Instead it was to be a highly circumscribed religious confession, confining Judaism into a more constricted space than it had ever previously occupied in the life of Jews.

Ernst Simon once made a distinction between 'catholic' and 'protestant' conceptions of the religion.[6] He defined as 'catholic' those religions which seek to sanctify all aspects of the life of the individual and the community – eating, drinking, work, rest, welfare and legislation, love and war.

'Protestant' were religions whose focus was on the individual, his direct relation to God and his personal faith and salvation. 'Protestant' religions arose when significant areas of public life became independent of ecclesiastical authority. Whether the distinction is accurate of Christianity, it is valuable in the case of Judaism. Modernity, for Jews, meant the protestantisation of a deeply catholic faith.

It created an identity crisis from which Jewry has not yet, two centuries later, fully recovered.[7] Its most obvious symptoms were assimilation and mixed marriage. Jewishness had been transformed from a state of being to a role,[8] and from destiny to conscious choice. In the neutral public space of a secular society, a Jew could for the first time choose to be something else without converting to another faith. It was a freedom of which, to a greater or lesser degree, many Jews availed themselves. The expansive horizons of modernity contrasted strongly with what seemed in retrospect to be the narrow confines of the ghetto. Jews could, quite simply, disappear. Many of them did.

In the attempt to stem the flow, a multitude of new definitions of Jewish existence appeared, among them Reform, Liberal, Conservative and Reconstructionist Judaisms, Hebrew and Yiddish culturalism, and secular Zionism. Some were consciously revolutionary, others sought a greater measure of continuity with the past. But the rabbinic tradition, which had held Jews together since the first century, had now become merely one way among others of being Jewish. It was now given the name 'Orthodoxy' by its critics, and its adherents declined with each passing year.

Despite the surge of activity – the nineteenth century witnessed more Judaic systems than the previous eighteen combined – an underlying note of pessimism is detectable in almost all the writings and speeches of this period. Jews and Judaism seemed scheduled for oblivion. At most, a secular nationalist identity might survive in what was to become the state of Israel. Religion had lost its power, and it was this alone that had provided Jews with their singular solidarity in dispersion. The voices of lamentation were heard from all directions. Orthodox leaders mourned the flight from tradition. Reformers were conscious of assimilation. Even the Yiddish and Hebrew poets, pioneers of a literary revival, asked whether there would be anyone left in the next generation to read their works.

The process did not affect all Jewish communities at the same time – the small Jewish townships of Eastern Europe were relatively undisturbed until the First World War – but it reached them all eventually. Often enough the bright hopes of civil equality, which first tempted Jews into abandoning their traditions, were soon overshadowed by the realisation that Enlightenment had not ended centuries of prejudice against Jews. It merely transformed a religious hatred into a secular one, as racial anti-semitism was born. Already by the closing decades of the nineteenth century, figures like Leon Pinsker and Theodor Herzl had concluded that the only safe place for Jews was away from Europe, in a land of their own. By 1945 their worst fears had been exceeded. The Holocaust had claimed among its victims one-third of the Jewish population of the world.

The combined effect of emancipation and attempted genocide seemed finally to have sealed the fate of Judaism. As late as 1967, the French sociologist, Georges Friedmann, wrote a book entitled *The End of the Jewish People?*[9] in which he argued that Jews now faced a simple choice: individual assimilation in the diaspora or collective assimilation in Israel. Intermarriage and the decline of religious observance meant the disappearance of Jews outside Israel, while Israel itself was a secular state which had severed its links with the religious past.

A PARTIAL REVIVAL

Whatever is the condition of Jews today, it is not what was expected. One example: In the early summer of this year, twenty thousand Jews gathered in Madison Square Garden to celebrate the completion of a seven year cycle of Talmud study. Not obviously an epoch-making event, until we recall that little over a century earlier, one of the great Jewish scholars of his day, Leopold Zunz, had predicted that by the twentieth century there would be no one left to understand a rabbinic text, while another, Moritz Steinschneider, had declared that his task was to give the remains of Judaism a decent burial.

Today there are more Jews studying in *yeshivot* – rabbinical seminaries – than at any time since the great Babylonian academies. Throughout the diaspora there is an unprecedented growth in institutions of Jewish education. In Israel itself, religious groups – tiny when the state was founded and believed by Ben Gurion to be a mere relic of the past – are a powerful political presence. The last strongholds of Jewish tradition in Central and Eastern Europe had been almost completely destroyed by the Holocaust. Today the survivors have almost miraculously repopulated themselves, and their centres flourish in Israel and America. Today's is the first generation of Orthodox Jews in two centuries to have witnessed growth, not decline.

Nor is it only within Orthodoxy that trends have been reversed. Since Israel's Six Day War in 1967, which had a dramatic effect on Jewish consciousness worldwide, the revival of identity has been widespread even among secular Jews. To be sure, this would probably be described as an ethnic rather than a religious phenomenon. But two points are worth making. First, ethnicity has proved strikingly resilient in societies like Britain and America, overturning previous assumptions of the assimilationist or melting-pot model of minority communities. Second, it is often surprisingly difficult to disentangle religious and secular motifs in ethnic cultures. It was Will Herberg's insight, in his *Protestant-Catholic-Jew*,[10] to note that in America a highly secularised form of religion had become the basis of ethnicity, as third generation immigrants sought a way of perpetuating identity that was more durable than the memories, manners and languages of Eastern Europe. The unexpected capacity of religious traditions to adjust to a secular culture – admittedly more pronounced in the United States than in Britain – has been a significant factor in their persistence.

These developments do not amount to a simple story of religious revival. The majority of Jews are highly secularised. In the United States, for example, a 1988 survey revealed that when asked about the qualities they considered most important to their Jewish identity, 59 per cent replied 'a commitment to social equality' while only 17 per cent answered 'religious observance.'[11] Since the mid-1980s an argument has raged between Jewish sociologists as to whether recent trends in American Jewry are evidence of the transformation of Judaism or its decline.[12] The facts support both an optimistic and pessimistic reading of the future of Jewish identity. The argument parallels the more general debate among sociologists as to how secularisation is to be assessed. A measure of how complex and confused the issue can be is given by the evidence of a recent survey among Jews, in which 91 per cent agreed that 'Without Jewish religion the Jewish people could not survive,' while two- thirds *disagreed* with the statement that 'To be a good Jew one must believe in God.'[13]

But one thing at least was clear from the Jewish case. The trajectory mapped out by Judaism in the late twentieth century has run counter to prediction. Jews have continued strongly to identify as Jews: much more than had seemed likely a century earlier. The nature of that survival is complex. While a small minority has become more religiously observant, the majority is content with increasingly attenuated forms of attachment. Only ten per cent of American Jews attend synagogue more than once a month. One in three marry outside the faith. Already in 1957 Nathan Glazer could speak of the 'stubborn insistence on remaining a Jew, enhanced by no particularly ennobling idea of what that means.'[14] Since then, that judgement could be slightly qualified. The 1967 Six Day War made Jews worldwide aware of the vulnerability of the state of Israel. It brought to the surface the repressed trauma of the Holocaust. Jewish survival took on the force of a moral imperative, a way of saying 'Never again' to what had happened during the Final Solution.[15] But in 1990 Glazer could repeat his caveat about the emptiness at the heart of contemporary Jewish existence: 'Jews survive,' he wrote, 'in order to survive.'[16]

And there lies the paradox. Religious identity can persist in the absence of religious belief. Were this a Jewish phenomenon only, it would not have fallen within the necessarily broader perspectives of the Reith Lectures. The subject I had chosen to address was, after all, not Judaism but religion itself in a secular society. But the Jewish case was not unique. It matched the experience of other religious and ethnic minorities since the 1960s. More significantly, it mirrored the paradox of a contemporary Britain in which the overwhelming majority of the population declare themselves to be Christian, yet rarely go to church. Religious attachments remain even in a society in which religious behaviour is measurably in decline. The question is: what is one to make of this fact?

RELIGIOUS IDENTITY AS MORAL POSSIBILITY

There are two obvious possible interpretations. One is that religion has, after all, persisted and that we are wrong to measure it solely by traditional indices such as attendance at a place of worship. The transformation of religion is not its eclipse. It remains, as Durkheim would have seen it, as the network of symbols and meanings that constitute society.[17] Alternatively, as Daniel Bell argued, it endures as 'the awareness of men of their finiteness and the inexorable limits to their powers, and the consequent effort to find a coherent answer to reconcile them to that human condition.'[18] Either way – as a feature of society or the individual – religion is, on this reading, a universal phenomenon. Man is a meaning-seeking animal, and there are therefore limits to the 'disenchantment of the world' and its reduction to that which can be perceived or controlled. Religion should not be confused with its classic institutional expressions. It survives through time, but it may take new and unexpected forms.

The other and opposite alternative is that religion as we have known it is in fact dying, and that such signs of life as it presently displays are only its death-pangs. As Bryan Wilson, the most persuasive and consistent advocate of this view has put it, 'It does not appear that men will be able to remake the world we have lost, and, unless there is a massive change of heart, a veritable revolution in thought and feeling .... it is difficult to see how the otherwise irrevocable pattern of societal order could be reinfused with religious inspiration.'[19]

Religion, then, is either alive and well or slowly and sometimes convulsively expiring. Both views have much to commend them. But I preferred a third way of approaching the subject, neither descriptive nor predictive but quite simply moral. Our religious commitments have indeed suffered a massive attrition. But they have not yet disappeared. And therein lies a momentous possibility. I was much impressed by something Nathan Glazer had written a quarter-century ago. He had noted the persistence of Jewish identity in an open society, and seen, too, that it was largely devoid of religious content. But he added this: 'The insistence of the Jews on remaining Jews, which may take the religiously indifferent forms of liking Yiddish jokes, supporting Israel, raising money for North African Jews, and preferring certain kinds of food, has a potentially religious meaning. It means that the Jewish religious tradition is not just a subject for scholars but is capable now and then of finding expression in life. And even if it finds no expression in one generation or another, the commitment to remain related to it still exists. Dead in one, two or three generations, it may come to life in the fourth.'[20]

What made Glazer different from other sociologists of religion is that he did not rest content with interpretation of the facts. He saw that they contained a moral, and even spiritual, possibility. That possibility may not yet have been realised. But that it exists makes our situation reversible. Secularisation is not a one-way street. Movement is possible in the opposite direction. And this to me, as a religious believer, not a sociologist, was the important conclusion.

In a culture which has become deeply secularised, some last embers of faith still glow. What we make of that fact depends on us as freely choosing agents. There is a point at which prediction ends and decision begins. But the choices available within a society are not open-ended. They depend on the resources available within its culture. My argument in these lectures was simply this: that religious values are still active within our frame of moral reference. They have been eroded but not altogether eclipsed. They lie at the heart of some of our deepest moral commitments: to the worth of the individual, to society as a covenant rather than as a contract, to morality itself as a communal endeavour, and to the family as the crucible of personal relationships. I see these as endangered but not unrecoverable institutions. Whether or not they logically require a religious base is not my concern here. Historically, religious communities have been their natural environment. Living, as we have done, by the inherited habits of an essentially religious way of life, we have come to underestimate the religious faith needed to sustain them. We have assumed that some secular foundation could be discovered on the basis of which they could be preserved. But it has thus far eluded us, and the prospects are not good.

COMMUNITY, TRADITION AND MORAL ECOLOGY

The connecting thread running through the lectures is the idea of religion as part of our moral and social ecology. That concept derives from Robert Bellah and the important study he, along with Richard Madsen, William Sullivan, Ann Swidler and Steven Tipton, produced of the state of contemporary America: *Habits of the Heart*.[21] The picture Bellah drew was of a society deeply fragmented by the prevailing individualism of a culture in which tradition and community were in a state of advanced deterioration. Bellah had long argued that 'any coherent and viable society rests on a common set of moral understandings about good and bad, right and wrong, in the realm of individual and social action,' and that 'these common moral understandings must also in turn rest upon a common set of religious understandings that provide a picture of the universe in terms of which the moral understandings make sense.'[22] By the mid-1980s, after five years of research into 'middle America,' he was able to chart the effects of their erosion across a whole series of domains: personal ambition, family relationships, citizenship and the sense of national community.

His conclusions were sombre and they applied equally, in my judgement, to British society. Expressive and utilitarian individualism had replaced, as modes of thought, the earlier biblical and republican traditions on which American society had grown to maturity. Those earlier 'habits of the heart' had tempered individualism with more expansive virtues. Like de Tocqueville a century and a half earlier, Bellah feared that the demise of religion as a vehicle of continuity and societal concern would leave the individual isolated and vulnerable and the moral fabric of the liberal state dangerously weakened. 'It has been evident for some time,' he wrote, 'that unless we begin to repair the damage to our social ecology, we will destroy ourselves long before natural ecological disaster has time to be realised.'[23]

What Glazer had seen to be possible, Bellah now declared necessary: a recovery of those essentially religious values, traditions and modes of life that had once linked individuals to the larger collective enterprise of society, and had forged links between past and present. It was this argument that I sought to develop in *The Persistence of Faith*. One aspect of it, in particular, needs spelling out if it is not to be misunderstood.

Implicit in these lectures is a critique of a tenacious modern fallacy: the omnipotence of politics, in the narrow sense of governments, policies and parties. Roughly speaking, this amounts to the view that the political system is the only significant vehicle of change in societies as secular as our own. Crime, addiction, education, environmental exploitation, even rates of marriage and divorce, are to be controlled, if at all, by government legislation. If religious groups have any contribution to make in this process, it is by way of issuing recommendations to governments or critiques of legislative and fiscal policy or by participating in the national debates that surround new enactments. At most they figure as one set of interests among many, and such influence as they wield has more to do with a vestigial deference towards religious leaders than with any real sway they hold over hearts and minds. The corollary of the omnipotence of politics is the impotence of religion.

I doubt whether any reflective politician today subscribes to this view, but its shortcomings are painfully apparent. Survey after survey reveals the extent to which social ills survive legislative attempts to cure them. Poverty, under achievement, educational standards, birthrates and rates of divorce are relatively resistant to government action, whether the state is pursuing a maximalist or minimalist course. The forces that shape a society lie too deep to be reached by any but the most totalitarian political regime; and totalitarianism is precisely what, in the late twentieth century, we would wish to avoid at any cost.

For some reason, analyses of American society – among them those of Bellah, Peter Berger, Daniel Bell, Lionel Trilling and Christopher Lasch – have had a more overtly cultural and religious dimension than their British counterparts. But their relevance spans the Atlantic. Underlying them is the assumption that there are institutions, modes of behaviour, structures of aspiration and 'habits of the heart' that are essential to the health of the *polls,* but which cannot be created by political means. Collectively these are what are meant by the phrase 'moral ecology.' They were, traditionally, the domain of religion. I believe they still are.

Great harm is done to the potential contribution of religion to social debates when the wider and narrower senses of 'the political' are confused. The great world religions cannot be reduced, without massive distortion, to party political programmes. There is something absurd and demeaning in conjecturing whether the sages, saints and prophets would have voted Labour or Conservative or whether they would have supported the free market or the welfare state. They were concerned with the *polis*, with what I have called the structures of our common life. But they were concerned with ends rather than means, with moral imperatives rather than economic interests, and with duties rather than rights. The truths they represented were not measurable by elections or opinion polls. But that is not to say that they do not have the deepest relevance to the wellbeing of a society, perhaps more so than the narrowly political decisions which tend to monopolise our attention.

I write, of course, from the Jewish – specifically the rabbinic – tradition. It was that tradition, with its emphasis on the family, education, philanthropy and the sanctification of everyday life, which between the first and nineteenth centuries shaped Jewish communities throughout the diaspora despite their almost total lack of political power. Judaism contains a distinctive and highly articulated vision of society, but it is not one that can be translated into conventional political categories. Its emphasis on community, compassion and social justice led one generation to identify Judaism with socialism. Its equally strong insistence on individual responsibility led another generation to identify it with the New Right and the minimalist state. But Judaism is not the one nor the other but a religious culture that encompasses both. Hillel, the pre-Christian rabbinic sage, put it well when he said, 'If I am not for myself, who will be? But if I am only for myself, what am I?'[24] Rabbinic Judaism is rich in teachings about the individual, the family and the religious community, but has little to say about the state. Its concern is with moral ecology: the environment within which a political system must work, rather than the system itself.

The kinship between this perspective and that invoked by Bellah and others writing within a Christian tradition convinced me that there was a truth to be explored that went beyond specific faiths and societies. At its simplest it is that there are deep-seated problems which have been wrongly identified as political as if they could be solved by government action alone. They are instead cultural, moral and ultimately religious and call for a religious response. I do not share the pessimism of Bryan Wilson who can stigmatise such an approach as 'a lingering rhetorical invocation in support of conventional morality ... a cry of despair in the face of moral panic.'[25] That judgement assumes that further secularisation is inevitable. There can be no constructive religious response, because faith has lost its power to change lives. Against that I believe that just as we have the ability to draw back from the abyss of ecological disaster, so we have the ability to change direction in the face of social disaster. A renewal of our religious traditions may be no more than a possibility, but it is no less, either.

THE ASSAULT ON TRADITIONS

But Bellah's argument was part of a far wider mood of cultural reconsideration, of which I hoped these lectures would be an approachable expression. Here of necessity I was drawn into a vast simplification of complex processes. It is difficult to compress three hundred years of moral philosophy into a half-hour radio talk, as I do in my second lecture, without feeling that some injustice has been done to the subject. The result can be, as Sam Goldwyn is reputed to have said, 'on the surface, profound, but deep down, superficial.' My mandate was the reply of Daniel Bell when asked by Professor T. H. Marshall, 'What do you specialise in?' Bell's answer was a model of *chutzpah*. 'I specialise,' he said, 'in generalisations.'

The generalisation which underlies my argument is this. The Enlightenment and the intellectual and social processes to which it gave rise have had a devastating effect on the traditions which give meaning and shape to life lived in community. They have focused relentlessly on two entities: the individual, detached from historical context, and the universal, politically realised in the secular state. They have left little space for that third essential component of our social ecology: particular and concrete communities of character, of which religions were and are the most potent examples.

To put it briefly and bluntly, neither the individual nor the state is where we discover who we are and why. Hegel believed that the state was the embodiment of moral community. A line of modern thinkers from Nietzsche to Sartre and the British analytical tradition has held that moral meanings are manufactured by the individual, a view that J. L. Mackie neatly summarised when he gave his book *Ethics* the subtitle, 'Inventing Right and Wrong.'[26] Neither of these views has serious viability. The modern state is too diverse and simply too large for a single richly articulated moral tradition, such as Hegel envisaged, to prevail. Nietzsche's view, on the other hand, dissolves morality altogether, a fact to which he was far more alive than the majority of his successors. Beyond the most basic rules necessary for the maintenance of the most rudimentary social order, morality lives in communities and the traditions which sustain them. And it was precisely such communities and traditions that Enlightenment sought to dissolve.

Once again, the Jewish experience is germane, and the example of Spinoza [1632–1677], the archetypal modern Jewish thinker, particularly so. The seventeenth century Amsterdam in which Spinoza grew up was home to an unusual group of Jews. From the fourteenth to the sixteenth centuries in Spain and Portugal, a large number of Jews, under coercion of various kinds, had converted to Christianity. Secretly, they remained loyal and practising Jews. They were known to the rabbis as *anusim*, forced converts, but to the Spanish they were the *marranos*: 'swine.' The marranos were caught in a classic double bind: to Jews they were betrayers of their ancestral faith, to Christians they were covert heretics. After the horrors of the Spanish Inquisition and expulsion, some of them sought freer air and turned among other places to Amsterdam. That background is essential to an understanding of Spinoza's thought.

Its effect is directly and radically to subvert traditional religious self-understanding. Excommunicated by the Jewish community in 1656, Spinoza proceeded in his *Tractatus Theologico-Politicus* and *Ethics* to argue that the Bible was a human document, and biblical law merely Moses' attempt at social engineering. One by one he demythologised the terms of religious experience. There were no such things as miracles or Providence. God was simply another way of conceiving nature so that the idea of a personal God was a confusion. Human freewill too was an illusion, as was the idea of man as something set apart from nature. The idea of moral responsibility, and with it praise and blame, rested on a fallacy. Like Freud, he insisted that people must be studied scientifically, as objects within nature, rather than as subjects within a culture.[27] In Spinoza we see, in Paul Johnson's apt description, the 'sheer destructive power of Jewish rationalism once it escaped the restraints of the traditional community.'[28]

So systematic a work of intellectual demolition has a social context. In Spinoza's case, it is a natural response to the impossible burden of marrano existence, doubly alienated from both Christian and Jewish identities.[29] The escape from conflicting traditions is to be found in a world where all traditions have been dissolved and human beings inhabit a neutral, value-free society governed by abstract reason alone. Nor was Spinoza's case exceptional. As emancipation gathered pace in the nineteenth century a great many intellectuals of Jewish origin found themselves caught between a past from which they believed themselves to have escaped and a present to which they had not yet secured admission. They were, in a sense, modern marranos.[30] Their fate had a wider significance because, including as they did Marx, Durkheim, Freud, Kafka, Wittgenstein and Levi-Strauss, they were among the shapers of the modern mind. Taken collectively, their work constitutes a massive relativisation of tradition and the dissolution of its claims on identity. It was their simultaneous exorcism of Judaism and a non-Jewish culture which still excluded Jews.

In a perceptive essay first published in 1919, Thorstein Veblen noted that 'It appears to be only when the gifted Jew escapes from the cultural environment created and fed by the particular genius of his own people ... that he comes into his own as a creative leader in the world's intellectual enterprise.' He becomes 'a disturber of the intellectual peace,' but only at the cost of becoming 'a wanderer in the intellectual No Man's Land.'[31] The marrano quality of the Jewish thinkers of the nineteenth and early twentieth centuries is reflected in that most characteristic vantage point of modernity, what Thomas Nagel called 'the view from nowhere,' standing outside all received and historically nurtured systems of meaning. Alasdair MacIntyre writes about the self of modern moral theory, that it 'has no necessary social content and no necessary social identity.' It 'can then be anything, can assume any role or take any point of view, because it *is* in and for itself nothing.'[32] No better description could have been given of the systematically alienated Jewish intellectuals who played no small part in creating the world of thought which MacIntyre describes.

TRADITION AND THE RECOVERY OF MEANING

The Jewish example is only an extreme case of what has happened to every traditional community that has experienced modernity. The world that thus emerges is of individuals as the makers of their own meanings, and of the state as the neutral arbitrator between conflicting interests. Religion then becomes a private affair in which – in the Christian theology of a Don Cupitt[33] or the Jewish thought of a Eugene Borowitz[34] – personal autonomy reigns supreme.

For a century or more this universe was incubated in the minds of intellectuals. But in the 1960s, in the West, it became a popular reality. Nietzsche's lofty transvaluation of values became a street slogan in the form of doing your own thing and choosing whatever works for you. Theologians became front page news as they endorsed the 'moral revolution' and the 'death of God.' No less a figure than Sir Edmund Leach began his 1967 Reith Lectures with the declaration that 'Men have become gods. Isn't it about time we understood our divinity?' Within a decade, traditional values had lost their legitimation. Peter Berger once noted that the word 'heresy' derives from the Greek *haeresis*, meaning choice. Once life becomes lifestyle and all morality a matter of choice, heresy has become, as it were, the air we breathe.[35] The central religious assumption that there are moral absolutes which are given, not chosen, has been sent into cultural exile.

We still live with the consequences of that revolution. But no sooner was it announced than the possibility of a counterrevolution became apparent. T. S. Eliot had defended the rootedness of the artist in the community of his or her predecessors in his seminal essay, 'Tradition and the Individual Talent.'[36] Martin Heidegger had, in his philosophy, stressed the fact that the individual is necessarily located in a history. There is no 'view from nowhere.' Ernst Gombrich had elegantly demonstrated, in his studies of the pictorial arts, that representation and expression could not be divorced from the traditions which formed the language within which the artist worked.[37] T. S. Kuhn overturned our understanding of the methods of science in his *The Structure of Scientific Revolutions*, showing that the questions scientists asked and the conclusions they drew were governed by prior expectations, themselves part of the prevailing traditions of the scientific community.[38]

Meanwhile, in hermeneutics Hans-Georg Gadamer had cast doubt on the idea of a detached reading of a text.[39] In biblical studies, Brevard Childs encouraged us to see the Bible from within the history of the community of faith.[40] Within sociology, Robert Bellah and Peter Berger counted the costs of modernity in terms of what Berger called 'the homeless mind.'[41] Above all, in philosophy, doubts began to be expressed about the direction of moral and political thought since the Enlightenment. The opening shots were fired by Alasdair MacIntyre in his *After Virtue*, published in 1981, in which he argued that though in our time 'the language and the appearances of morality persist,' in fact 'the integral substance of morality has to a large degree been fragmented and then in part destroyed.' Since then, such major figures as Charles Taylor, Michael Walzer, Michael Sandel and Stuart Hampshire have all added to our understanding of the role of particular traditions as against abstract rationality in ethics.[42]

Clearly, such diverse figures were not all saying the same thing. But they amounted to a significant, perhaps Copernican, shift in intellectual mood. In their various ways they were calling into question some of the deepest assumptions of the Enlightenment, above all its focus on the individual and the universal. They were reminding us that our meanings are *neither* individual *nor* universal, but belong to communities and the traditions that inform them. The human situation is not exhausted by individual choice on the one hand or universal reason on the other. We understand our world through the particular given of our historical situation. After a century in which homelessness seemed to be the natural condition of intellectuals, here were thinkers attempting to recover a sense of at-homeness. Collectively they posed the question: can we reinstate tradition?

Nor was this a movement among academics alone. There have been other and broader symptoms of a shift in the direction of society. The social correlate of Enlightenment universalism was assimilation. Minority groups would melt and merge into the archetype of the citizen in general. Since the 1960s, that model has been progressively displaced by resurgent ethnicity and cultural pluralism. We have come to see minority traditions as cultures which it is important to preserve. No less importantly, conservative religious groups have shown immense vigour during this period. It has been as if, bewildered by the surfeit of choice, we have longed for lost moral certainties. And there has been renewed interest, stimulated by the pioneering work of Peter Berger and Richard Neuhaus,[43] in mediating structures, those associations like the family, the local community and the religious congregation, that stand between the individual and the state and provide us with our most enduring sense of identity. We have begun to ask how they can be protected.

The analogy between social and physical ecology is striking. In the 1980s, precisely as green issues came to dominate the political agenda, so were voices raised in protest at the damage we have done to our moral environment. Alasdair MacIntyre ended *After Virtue* with a warning about 'the coming ages of barbarism and darkness.'[44] Bryan Wilson concluded his study of secularisation, *Religion in Sociological Perspective*,[45] with the question, 'Without trust, without mutuality, with only reduced and fragile possibilities for enduring relationships, how will those minimal requirements of even the most rational system be met?' Robert Bellah ended *Habits of the Heart*[46] with the remark that 'we are hovering on the very brink of disaster, not only from international conflict but from the internal incoherence of our own society.' These prophetic utterances, breaking through the usual constraints of academic discourse, were urging with great passion that in losing our religious traditions we had eroded that environment within which alone a cohesive intellectual, social, political and moral life is possible. We had reached the limits of the processes set in motion by the Enlightenment, and we had now somehow to construct a post-modern world that would recover the restraints, commitments and loyalties of the pre-modern past. It was these voices to which I sought to give expression in the lectures that follow.

That, then, was my starting point. We are nearing the end of a period in human civilisation in which there seemed to be no limits to individual choice and collective progress. Traditions had been deconstructed and technical reason took their place. Ends were things we individually chose, and the machinery of science and government provided the means. Within this promethean vision, religion could lead at most a diminishing and marginal existence.

But already this social and intellectual world has lost its plausibility. Enlightenment ended in Holocaust. Economic growth threatens the environment. Above all, the erosion of our structures of relationship and meaning has left us with that sense of being cast adrift in an impersonal social order that Emile Durkheim called anomie. The signs of our seeking something else are present in the revival of ethnic and religious loyalties, often subtly intertwined.

We are caught between two ages, one passing, the other not yet born, and the conflicting tendencies we witness – deepening secularisation on the one hand, new religious passions on the other – are evidence of the transition. The next chapter in the story is impossible to predict. But I argue this, that we have not yet reflected sufficiently on how to renew our religious commitments and with them our most basic social institutions, and that in an age of transition there is a great danger of secular and religious extremisms creating conflicts for which we are ill prepared. The discontents of modernity run high, and there are already signs of sharp cultural clashes – most obviously within Islam, but within Christianity and Judaism also – between modernists and neotraditionalists.

I have tried in these lectures to state the case for a broadly based return to tradition within the context of religious pluralism and tolerance. But I do not believe that the balance between conflicting forces will be easy to achieve. Ecological catastrophe can only be avoided at the cost of significant restraints on all sides; and that holds true of social ecology also. I believe that religious values remain a potent enough force within our culture to be renewed. And I believe that for our society to remain viable they must be renewed.

NOTES

1   Alexis de Tocqueville, *Democracy in America*, London: Fontana, 1968, 1: 364.

2   Quoted in Norman Dennis and A. H. Halsey, *English Ethical Socialism*, Oxford: Clarendon Press, 1988, 19.

3   Bryan Wilson, 'Secularization,' in *The Encyclopaedia of Religion*, edited by Mircea Eliade, New York: Macmillan, 1987.

4   Peter Berger, *The Sacred Canopy*, New York: Doubleday, 1967, 107.

5   Bryan Wilson, 'Secularization: The Inherited Model,' in Phillip E. Hammond (ed.), *The Sacred in a Secular Age*, Berkeley: University of California Press, 1985, 20.

6   Ernst Simon, 'Are We Israelis Still Jews?' in Arthur A. Cohen (ed.), *Arguments and Doctrines*, New York: Harper and Row, 1970, 388-401.

7   Some of the dimensions of this are charted in Jonathan Sacks, *Traditional Alternatives*, London: Jews' College Publications, 1989; *Tradition in an Untraditional Age*, London: Vallentine Mitchell, 1990; and *One People?*, Oxford: Oxford University Press/Littman Library, forthcoming.

8   See Peter Berger and Thomas Luckmann, *The Social Construction of Reality*, Harmondsworth: Penguin, 1987, 108–109.

9   Georges Friedmann, *The End of the Jewish People?*, London: Hutchinson, 1967.

10 Will Herberg, *Protestant-Catholic-Jew*, New York, Doubleday, 1955.

11 Quoted by Seymour Martin Lipset, 'A Unique People in an Exceptional County,' in Seymour Martin Lipset (ed.), *American Pluralism and the Jewish Community*, New Brunswick: Transaction Publishers, 1990, 20.

12 There is, by now, a large literature on the subject. See especially, Steven M. Cohen, *American Assimilation or Jewish Revival?*, Bloomington: Indiana University Press, 1988; Calvin Goldscheider, *Jewish Continuity and Change*, Bloomington: Indiana University Press, 1986; Charles Liebman, *Deceptive Images*, New Brunswick: Transaction Books, 1988; Charles E. Silberman, *A Certain People*, New York: Summit, 1985.

13 Quoted in Nathan Glazer, 'American Jewry or American Judaism,' Seymour Martin Lipset, op. cit., 35.

14 Nathan Glazer, *American Judaism*, Chicago: University of Chicago Press, 1957, 143.

15 The most sophisticated philosophical statement of this new mood is contained in Emil Fackenheim, *The Jewish Return into History*, New York: Schocken Books, 1978.

16 Nathan Glazer, 'American Jewry or American Judaism,' 35.

17 See, for example, Thomas Luckmann, *The Invisible Religion*, New York: Macmillan, 1967.

18 Daniel Bell, 'The Return of the Sacred? The Argument on the Future of Religion,' *British Journal of Sociology* 28:4 (December 1977), 447.

19 Bryan Wilson, *Religion in Sociological Perspective*, Oxford: Oxford University Press, 1982, 179.

20 Glazer, *American Judaism*, 144.

21 Robert Bellah, Richard Madsen, William M. Sullivan, Ann Swidler and Steven M. Tipton, *Habits of the Heart: Middle America Observed*, London: Hutchinson, 1988.

22 *Robert N. Bellah*, The Broken Covenant: American Civil Religion in Time of Trial, *New York: Seabury Press, 1975, ix.*

23 Habits of the Heart, *284.*

24   Mishnah, *Avot* 1:14.

25   Bryan Wilson, 'Secularization: The Inherited Model,' 19.

26   J. L. Mackie, *Ethics: Inventing Right and Wrongs* Harmondsworth: Penguin, 1977.

27   See Stuart Hampshire, *Spinoza*, Harmondsworth: Penguin, 1965.

28   Paul Johnson, *A History of the Jews,* London: Weidenfeld and Nicolson, 1988, 291–2.

29   See Yirmiyahu Yovel, *Spinoza and Other Heretics*, Princeton: Princeton University Press, 1989, and Michael Wyschogrod, *The Body of Faith*, Minneapolis: Seabury Press, 1983, 40–81.

30   See John Murray Cuddihy, *The Ordeal of Civility,* Boston: Beacon Press, 1987.

31   Thorstein Veblen, 'The Intellectual Pre-eminence of Jews in Modern Europe,' *Political Science Quarterly* 34 (March 1919), 33–42.

32   Alasdair MacIntyre, *After Virtue*, London: Duckworth, 1981, 30.

33   Don Cupitt, *The Sea of Faith*, London: BBC, 1984.

34   Eugene B. Borowitz, *Choices in Modern Jewish Thought,* New York: Behrman House, 1983.

35   Peter Berger, *A Rumour of Angels,* London: Allen Lane, 1970, 62.

36   T. S. Eliot, 'Tradition and the Individual Talent,' in *Selected Essays,* London: Faber and Faber, 1976, 13–22.

37   E. H. Gombrich, *Art and Illusion,* Oxford: Phaidon Press, 1988.

38   T. S. Kuhn, *The Structure of Scientific Revolutions,* Chicago: University of Chicago Press, 1970.

39   Hans-Georg Gadamer, *Truth and Method,* New York: Crossroad, 1985.

40   B. S. *Childs,* Introduction to the Old Testament as Scripture, *London: SCM, 1979.*

41   Peter Berger, Brigitte Berger and Hansfried Kellner, *The Homeless Mind*, Harmondsworth: Penguin, 1973.

42   See Stuart Hampshire, *Morality and Conflict*, Oxford: Blackwell, 1983; Michael Sandel, *Liberalism and the Limits of Justice*, Cambridge: Cambridge University Press, 1982; Michael Sandel (ed.), *Liberalism and its Critics*, Oxford: Blackwell, 1984; Michael Walzer, *Spheres of Justice*, Oxford: Blackwell, 1983; Richard J. Bernstein, *Beyond Objectivism and Relativism*, Oxford: Blackwell, 1983; Jeffrey Stout, *Ethics After Babel*, Boston: Beacon Press, 1988; Charles

Taylor, *Hegel and Modern Society*, Cambridge: Cambridge University Press, 1979; *Philosophy and the Human Sciences*, Cambridge: Cambridge University Press, 1985; *Sources of the Self*, Cambridge: Cambridge University Press, 1989.

43 Peter Berger and Richard Neuhaus, *To Empower People*, Washington D.C.: American Enterprise Institute, 1977.

44 After Virtue, *244.*

45 Religion in Sociological Perspective, *177–178.*

46 Habits of the Hearty, *284.*

I

THE ENVIRONMENT OF FAITH

There are moments when you can see the human landscape change before your eyes, and 1989 was one of them. In retrospect it will seem as significant a turning point in history as 1789, the year of the French revolution and the birth of the secular state. Throughout Eastern Europe, in one country after another, Communism appeared to crumble. The twentieth century had broken its greatest idols, the two versions of an absolute secular state: Fascism, defeated in 1945, and East European Communism which expired last year. But what, in this revolution of the human spirit, lies ahead?

In the middle of it all, the American historian Francis Fukuyama wrote an article entitled, 'The End of History?'[1] In it he described the global spread of liberal democracy not as the triumph of an ideal, but as the victory of consumer culture. In the end, colour television had proved a more seductive prospect than the Communist Manifesto. Politics had moved beyond ideology. As Edward Shevardnadze, the Soviet Foreign minister, put it, 'the struggle between two opposing systems' had been superseded by the desire 'to build up material wealth at an accelerated rate.' Dialectical materialism was over; mail-order catalogue materialism had taken its place. Eastern Europe had discovered the discreet charm of the bourgeoisie.

It was, said Fukuyama, the end of history as we had known it: the struggle over ideas that had once called forth daring, courage and imagination. Instead we would increasingly see societies based on nothing but the free play of choices and interests. What would absorb the human imagination would no longer be large and visionary goals but 'economic calculation, the endless solving of technical problems, environmental concerns, and the satisfaction of sophisticated consumer demands.' History would end not with the sound of apocalypse but the beat of a personal stereo.

Fukuyama's analysis takes us deep into irony, because such a brave new world without ideals suggests a massive impoverishment of what we are as human beings. Its accuracy as a prediction is matched only by its narrowness as a prescription. The human being as consumer neither is nor can be all we are, and a social system built upon that premise will fail. The East has engaged in self-examination and has turned for inspiration to the West. But the West has yet to return the compliment and ask whether its own social fabric is in a state of good repair.

I believe it is not. And the problem lies not with our economic and political systems, but in a certain emptiness at the heart of our common life. Something has been lost in our consumer culture: that sense of meaning beyond ourselves that was expressed in our great religious traditions. It is not something whose eclipse we can contemplate with equanimity. Religious faith is central to a humane social order. To paraphrase a rabbinic saying: if we have only a secular society, even a secular society we will not have.

For some years we have known that unrestricted pursuit of economic growth has devastated our physical environment. Pollution, waste and the depletion of natural resources have disturbed that 'narrow strip of soil, air and water ... in which we live and move and have our being.'[2] No one intended it. It happened. But having happened, we can no longer ignore it. Whether our political commitments are blue, orange or red, we have all gone green. We have become aware that there are limits to growth.

But as well as a physical ecology, we also inhabit a moral ecology, that network of beliefs, relationships and virtues within which we think, act and discover meaning. For the greater part of human history it has had a religious foundation. But for the past two centuries, in societies like Britain, that basis of belief has been profoundly eroded. And we know too much about ecological systems to suppose that you can remove one element and leave the rest unchanged. There is, if you like, a God-shaped hole in our ozone layer. And it is time that we thought about moral ecology too.

THE PRIVATISATION OF FAITH

I speak from within the Jewish tradition, in which religion is more than 'what the individual does with his own solitude.'[3] God enters society in the form of specific ways of life, disclosed by revelation, mediated by tradition, embellished by custom and embodied in institutions. Faith lives not only in the privacy of the soul but in compassion and justice: the structures of our common life. The Hebrew Bible and the rabbis saw society as a covenant with God, and morality as a Divine imperative. That tradition has deep echoes in Christianity and Islam as well, and has shaped our moral imagination. To it we owe our ideas of the dignity of the individual as the image of God, and the sanctity of human life. It underlies our belief that we are free and responsible, not merely the victims of necessity and chance. And if we think of society as the place where we realise a vision of the good, somewhere behind that thought lies the influence of Exodus and Deuteronomy and Amos and Isaiah.

But one of the most powerful assumptions of the twentieth century is that faith is not like that. It belongs to private life.

Religion and society are two independent entities, so that we can edit God out of the language and leave our social world unchanged. After all, the whole history of the modern mind has been marked by the progressive detachment of knowledge from religious tradition. We no longer need, nor would we even think of invoking, God in order to understand nature or history. That battle was fought and lost by religion in the nineteenth century. But if what we know about ourselves and the world is independent of God, what difference could it make whether or not we still had religious faith? It might make all the difference to the private mind of the believer, but in the public world in which we act and interact, it should make no difference at all.

It was in the 1960s that we discovered how false this was. It was then that radical theologians took perverse pleasure in reciting that God – at least as we had known Him – was dead. But far from making no difference, it made a very great difference indeed. Because it was just then, in the decade of doing your own thing, that morality began to seem simply a matter of personal choice. A moral revolution was announced. In 1967 Sir Edmund Leach began his Reith Lectures with the words, 'Men have become gods. Isn't it about time we understood our own divinity?'[4] A massive shift was taking place in our public culture. Something was lost which we have not yet replaced. Faith and society turned out to be connected after all. If the idea of God was in eclipse, so was the way of life which it served as a foundation. The biblical tradition and its hierarchy of values had lost their persuasive power. And for a moment, rather than lament the fact, we enjoyed our liberation.

The sixties were probably the last time revolution could be sung to so cheerful a tune. Since then we have become increasingly aware of some of the problems of our social ecology: the urban slums, pollution, broken families and residual poverty which seem to yield neither to the welfare state nor to the minimalist state. We are less sure than we were that the future will be better than the past, that economic growth is open-ended or that utopia can be brought by any sort of revolution. So long as confidence in human progress remained high, religious belief seemed a dispensable commodity. But that optimism has now been shattered. Technology, which seemed to give man godlike powers of creation, has given him also demonic possibilities of destruction. Our loss of a shared morality has fragmented our social world and made even our most intimate relationships seem fragile and conditional. The question is: what moral resources have we left to lend us faith in difficult times? And the answer surely is: far fewer in Fukuyama's consumer culture than there are in the biblical tradition. We cannot edit God out of the language and leave our social world unchanged.

RELIGIOUS RESIDUES

But is Britain yet a post-religious society? Suppose that you had just landed in Britain for the first time and you wanted to know whether you had arrived in a religious country. What signs would you see? You would certainly see some. Here and there you would notice large religious buildings, mainly churches and cathedrals, whose intricate grandeur suggested considerable prestige. You would discover that religious leaders, bishops in particular, were quoted in the newspapers and sat in the House of Lords. You would be struck by the fact that a large number of businesses stopped on Sunday and asking why would receive an explanation that could hardly fail to mention Christianity. You might stop to ask why so many people were called John or David or Sarah or Elizabeth and learn that these were originally figures in the Bible. Inquiring, you would find that four in five Britons still regard themselves as Christian, that there are ethnic minorities where different traditions are still strong, and that only a tiny minority of the population describe themselves as atheists or agnostics. You might conclude that you had arrived in a religious society.

But you could hardly fail to notice different indicators as well. Examining the city skyline, you might well suspect that the true cathedrals of the urban landscape are office blocks. You would notice that the arenas where crowds gathered and formed temporary communions were football matches and pop concerts. You would see far fewer people engaged in spiritual exercises than in physical exercises. And if you came across individuals in solitary meditation, they would probably be watching a video rather than reading the Book of Common Prayer. You might be perplexed that so many churches had so few people in them; that there were urban areas where fewer than one in a hundred attended church on Sunday. And you would be struck by the fact that the largest crowds visiting cathedrals were tourists, not worshippers. Religion might be, in Stevie Smith's words, not waving but drowning.

What would you make of it all? You would, I think, rightly conclude that these survivals of religion were just that: survivals, residues of an earlier age in which religious institutions played a far greater part in our culture than they do today. But you might notice this as well. That places of worship were not quite yet museums. Inside them, you were not an observer or spectator only. You participated. They were perhaps the one place left where you stood in a living relationship with the past.

How was it, then, that religion, so central a component of the culture of the past, has come to be so marginal in the present? The story is part intellectual, part social. There was the rise of experimental science in the seventeenth century, the discovery that you could find out more about the world by observing it and framing hypotheses that could be tested, than by relying on past traditions: what Don Cupitt calls the shift from myths to maths.[5] There were the revolutionary changes in the way human beings were perceived: Spinoza's insistence that man too is a part of nature and subject to its laws, Marx's suggestion that our ideas are the product of economic forces, and Darwin's discovery that, as someone once put it, man's family tree goes back to the time when his ancestors were swinging from it. Individually, these weakened the hold of the narrative in the first chapter of Genesis in which man was created in the image of God. Collectively, they suggested the power of free inquiry as against the authority of ancient texts, when it came to the pursuit of knowledge.

The biblical tradition, far from being able to stand aside from these developments, eventually came under their scrutiny. Once thinkers were able to distance themselves from religion's claims, they were able to see it as a phenomenon to be explained like any other, in terms of economics or psychology, the projection onto heaven of human interests and needs. The supernatural had a natural explanation, and this weakened the idea of a Divine intrusion into the human domain, immune to the relativities of time. The ideas, central to the Bible, of revelation, miracle and redemption were undermined.

These intellectual developments went hand in hand with a transformation of society. It was difficult to see truth as timeless when the world was embarked on a roller-coaster of change. The industrial revolution broke up old crafts and communities and the traditions that went with them. And it changed the way people began to think about religion's most potent domain: ethics, or how to behave. An ethic which took science as its model would focus not on precedent but on consequences. Actions, like hypotheses, could be tested. The best were those that produced the greatest happiness for the greatest number. All this meant a quite tangible shift in the direction of human thought, from past to future, from essence to function, from virtue to pragmatism, and from passivity to control. Not only were the communities disrupted in which religious traditions had been lived and transmitted, but the entire cast of mind in which biblical ideas found a home had now gone. Consciousness had been secularised.

LIBERATION OR PRIVATION?

Throughout it all, with few dissenting voices, the consensus was that it was a journey of moral progress. But as they used to say in Yiddish: if things are so good, how come they're so bad? Because our modern conviction that man is a part of nature, subject to its laws, is more like paganism than the Biblical view of human dignity. The idea, which has gained great power in recent decades, that human life is dispensable through abortion or euthanasia looks more like a regression than a moral advance. And the notion that authenticity means making our own rules is the loss of a world of value beyond the self. Surely the crucial biblical insight was that something else might be true: that man, gifted with language and thus imagination, might seek meaning in the midst of chaos and come to experience it in the form of a moral call not implicit within nature but beyond. We might well feel that the whole thrust of the scientific imagination when applied to human culture was not so much to elevate man to the status of a god, but to reduce him to the quintessence of dust and brand all else an illusion. If so, we would have had our first intimation that what seemed so liberating about a post-religious age might be no more than a narrowing of human possibilities.

But only the first. For the fact, almost too obvious to need restating, is that not only have technological societies not replaced religious belief with some new overarching canopy of meaning, but in principle they could not do so. The very growth of modern knowledge has come about through specialisation and compartmentalisation, so that an integrated universe linking man and the cosmos is now beyond us. The more we know collectively, the less we know individually. Each of us understands very little of our world.

Not only that. The productive and social changes of the last two centuries have vastly multiplied our choices. Long gone are the days when our identities, beliefs, and life chances were narrowly circumscribed by where and to whom we happened to be born. We are no longer actors in a play written by tradition and directed by community, in which roles are allocated by accidents of birth. Instead careers, relationships and lifestyles have become things we freely choose from a superstore of alternatives.

Modernity is the transition from fate to choice. But at the same time it dissolves the commitments and loyalties that once lay behind our choices. Technical reason has made us masters of matching means to ends. But it has left us inarticulate as to why we should choose one end rather than another. The values that once led us to regard one as intrinsically better than another – and which gave such weight to words like good and bad – have disintegrated, along with the communities and religious traditions in which we learned them. Now we choose because we choose. Because it is what we want; or it works for us; or it feels right to me. Once we have dismantled a world in which larger virtues held sway, what remain are success and self-expression, the key values of an individualistic culture.

But can a society survive on so slender a moral base? The question was already raised in the nineteenth century by figures like Alexis de Tocqueville and Max Weber, who saw most clearly the connection between modern liberal democracies and the Judaeo-Christian tradition. It was de Tocqueville who saw that religion tempered individualism and gave those engaged in the competitive economy a capacity for benevolence and self-sacrifice. And it was he who saw that this was endangered by the very pursuit of affluence that was the key to economic growth.[6] Max Weber delivered the famous prophetic warning that the cloak of material prosperity might eventually become an iron cage. It was already becoming an end in itself, and other values were left, in his words, 'like the ghost of dead religious beliefs.'[7] Once capitalism consumed its religious foundations, both men feared the consequences.

The stresses of a culture without shared meanings are already mounting, and we have yet to count the human costs. We see them in the move from a morality of self-imposed restraint to one in which we increasingly rely on law to protect us from ourselves. In the past, disadvantaged groups could find in religion what Karl Marx called 'the feeling of a heartless world.' A purely economic order offers no such consolations. A culture of success places little value on the unsuccessful. The erosion of those bonds of loyalty and love which religion undergirded has left us increasingly alone in an impersonal economic and social system. Emile Durkheim was the first to give this condition a name. He called it anomie: the situation in which individuals have lost their moorings in a collective order. It is the heavy price we pay for our loss of communities of faith.

Fukuyama described a future dedicated to 'economic calculation, the endless solving of technical problems, environmental concerns and the satisfaction of sophisticated consumer demands.' But is such a world socially viable? Not all human problems are purely technical. One above all is not: the search for meaning which gave rise to the religious imagination in the first place.

THE BIBLICAL TRADITION

I have called the biblical tradition part of our moral ecology, by which I mean that until recently the language of British and American politics was rich in biblical themes: covenant and kinship, exodus and liberation, human dignity and responsibility. A religious vision could inspire Edmund Burke to conservatism, William Cobbett to socialism, and wend its variations from Thomas Jefferson to Martin Luther King. At times it spoke of the duty of the state to the individual, at others of the freedom of the individual against the state. It was a language, not a party political programme. But it was a distinctive language, quite unlike the vocabulary of a consumer culture, in which we speak only of rights and entitlements, interests and choices, self-expression and success.

It referred to meanings beyond the self, to moral communities beyond the individual and to relationships more enduring than temporary compatibility. It was a language that linked private faith to public action. It brought together what modernity has split asunder: society and the self. It was this tradition that led the great talmudist Rabbi Hayyim of Brisk to define the role of a religious leader as 'to redress the grievances of those who are abandoned and alone, to protect the dignity of the poor, and to save the oppressed from the hands of his oppressor.'[8] It moved one of Judaism's greatest mystics, Rabbi Menahem Mendel of Kotzk, to say that someone else's material concerns are my spiritual concerns.

But it is just this that leads me to believe that Fukuyama's prediction has not yet come to pass. For we still see other people's suffering and poverty not as things that merely happen in an impersonal order, but as things we ought somehow to relieve. They are, for us, *moral* issues. We do not see ourselves as consumers only, but as agents addressed by ethical imperatives. And for as long as we do so, we have moved beyond a view of society as the free play of interests. It remains for us a moral enterprise, actualising its values through history, the end point of which is redemption or, in Aharon Lichtenstein's fine phrase, collective beatitude.[9] We are back in the language of justice and compassion, words we once learned from the Bible and which led us to construct the society we have.

Which leads in turn to a significant conclusion: that though our churches and synagogues are underattended, people have not stopped identifying themselves as religious individuals, and have not yet stopped thinking in religious ways. However attenuated, the attachments remain. And this means more than that religion is for us a matter of nostalgia, or habit, or memories of grandparents and a simpler way of life. It means that it still remains for us a possibility. We are capable of being moved by calls to our conscience, to acts that make no sense in terms of self-fulfilment or private ambition. We have not yet lost the language of older and larger visions of the shared redemptive enterprise. We have it because the biblical tradition survives in our culture – marginal, endangered, a survival to be sure, but still there. Reminding us that the rules we make are subject to the rules we did not make, and that the making of moral history is not yet at an end.

NOTES

1 Francis Fukuyama, 'The End of History?' *The National Interest* (Summer 1989), 3–17.

2 John Passmore, *Man's Responsibility for Nature*, London: Duckworth, 1980, 3.

3 The phrase is taken from W. R. Inge.

4 E. R. Leach, *A Runaway World*, London, 1968.

5 Don Cupitt, *The Sea of Faiths* London: BBC, 1984, 31.

6 Alexis de Tocqueville, *Democracy in America*, translated by George Lawrence, London: Collins, 1968.

7 Max Weber, *The Protestant Ethic and the Spirit of Capitalism*, translated by Talcott Parsons, London: Unwin, 1987, 182.

8 Quoted in Rabbi Joseph B. Soloveitchik, *Halakhic Man*, translated by Lawrence Kaplan, Philadelphia: Jewish Publication Society of America, 1983, 91.

9 Aharon Lichtenstein, 'Religion and State: The Case for Interaction,' in Arthur A. Cohen (ed.), *Arguments and Doctrines: A Reader of Jewish Thinking in the Aftermath of the Holocaust*, New York: Harper and Row, 1970, 423.

2

DEMORALISATION

Voltaire, that eighteenth-century scourge of religion, used to refuse to let his friends discuss atheism in front of the servants. Unbelief was one thing between consenting intellectuals in private. But if it spread through society, morality would collapse. 'I want,' he said, 'my lawyer, tailor, valets, even my wife to believe in God. I think that if they do I shall be robbed less and cheated less.'[1]

For the greater part of human history, religion has been seen as the foundation of morality. In Dostoevsky's words: If God did not exist, all would be permitted. But this belief must seem to us now decidedly strange. Whether or not we believe in God, we inhabit a culture in which religious teachings are marginal to many people's moral choices. When did we last hear, in a television discussion or a newspaper editorial, the simple assertion that something was wrong because God or religious doctrine said so? Even a religious leader who said this in the course of public debate would nowadays be branded a fundamentalist. Our moral language has been effectively secularised. Religion enters our conversations obliquely and with embarrassment. Yet society survives. The world continues uninterrupted on its course. What is hard for us to understand in retrospect is how anyone could have thought otherwise.

But they did: believers and unbelievers alike. No one more so than the man who more than anyone severed morality from religion: Friedrich Nietzsche. Nietzsche was an unequalled critic of the Judaeo-Christian ethical tradition. But he did not believe that there could be a smooth transition to a secular morality. On the contrary, there would have to be a transvaluation of all values, a complete redefinition of our mental universe. It was necessary but it would be a nightmare. And in a famous passage Nietzsche imagines the speech of the madman who announces to a secular world that God is dead and we have killed him: 'What did we do when we unchained this earth from its sun? ... Are we not plunging continually? ... Are we not straying as through an infinite nothing?'² That is what it would feel like to lose the Divine foundations of our moral world. Within a few years of writing those lines Nietzsche went insane and shortly thereafter died.

What is it these thinkers saw that we fail to see? How were religion and morality associated in the first place? And how then, being thought inseparable, did they come to be separated? Above all, what happened to that predicted but strangely invisible tragedy, Voltaire's collapse of the social order, Nietzsche's infinite nothing?

GOD AND THE GOOD

The traditional connection between God and human goodness was straightforward. Revelation was legislation. Heaven had revealed what is right and what is wrong, and if it had not done so, how would we know? It is not that we would lack an answer. It is, rather, that we would have too many answers. We would arrive at the situation described at the end of the book of Judges, each person doing that which is right in his own eyes. What is more, the Law-giver was also the

Law-enforcer. God's existence guaranteed that the righteous would be rewarded and that evil would be repaid with evil. This answered the question that so troubled Plato: why be good if you can get away with being bad? An all-knowing, all-powerful God ensured that there would be no tax evaders in the kingdom of heaven. So religion underwrote the terms of morality. The knowledge of God led to virtue and the Day of Judgement put a heavy price on vice.[3]

But for the past several centuries that view has come increasingly under attack, for reasons that now seem quite clear. God may well have revealed a moral code. But it turned out to be a different moral code for Catholics and Protestants and Muslims and Jews. If we are to sort out what human beings *as such* should do, we will need something other than revelation. Besides which, as Kant suggested, if you try to get people to be good by rewarding them if they are and punishing them if they are not, you do not actually succeed in getting them to be good. You merely succeed in getting them to be pragmatic.[4] Then again, though this had been noted long before by Abraham and Jeremiah and Job, the view that the world was ruled by God on the principle of justice was difficult to reconcile with the facts. Evil prospered, the righteous for the most part suffered, and virtue had to be content with being its own reward. For people of faith this only served to show how inscrutable Divine justice was. But for those who brought less commitment to bear on the question, it was difficult to see how inscrutable justice was not another name for highly scrutable *in*justice.

None of these considerations was conclusive in itself. But by the seventeenth century other factors were at play. There was the morally ambivalent record of religion itself: its holy wars and persecutions. There was the rise of science as a competing source of knowledge to revelation. And perhaps above all there was that crucial transition by which, in Lionel Trilling's phrase, 'men became individuals.'[5] It is impossible to pinpoint when and why the first person singular moved into independent orbit. But we can detect significant moments: when writers embarked on the new literary form of autobiography; when Rembrandt started painting his long series of self-portraits; when Shakespeare has Polonius say to Laertes, 'This above all: to thine own self be true.' By the seventeenth century the idea of the individual as a reality in itself, apart from its social roles, was beginning to emerge. Whatever the cause, the consequence was clear. The independent self was about to change the course of moral thought.

At some point the revolutionary idea was born that religion, far from enhancing our moral development, significantly obstructs it. It kept us in a state of dependency. It took away from us the need, through trial and error, to find things out for ourselves. We became restless with a demanding Father who dictated the terms of our existence. Religion made us moral children, and if we were to reach maturity we would have to do without it. This idea, given its fullest expression by Freud, lies at the heart of three centuries of moral reflection: in the slow movement from virtue to authenticity, from morality as something objectively present in nature and society to something authored by the sovereign self.

It began with Spinoza, excommunicated by the Jewish community of Amsterdam in 1656: an outsider in a community of outsiders. Spinoza saw all religions as human constructs. The legislation of the Bible was not God's law but Moses' invention to turn a group of slaves into a nation. 'This then,' he said, 'was the object of the ceremonial law, that men should do nothing of their own free will, but should always act under external authority.'[6] In that sentence we hear the distinctive modern accent of the individual no longer shaped by, but now set over and against, religious commands. Its echoes were taken up and amplified by Kant, who insists that being moral cannot be a matter of submission to an external authority. It must be something that we impose on ourselves in what he called autonomy. Hegel went further in seeing the Hebrew Bible as the product of a slave mentality. And with an air of Samson pulling the temple down on the Philistines, Nietzsche demolished the whole structure of Judaeo-Christian ethics as a pious fraud: the bonds placed by the weak upon the strong.

Not all these figures were moral revolutionaries. Kant in particular had a high regard for traditional morality and believed that he was merely underpinning it with more solid foundations. But radical consequences were to follow. Once morality was divorced from a theistic vision of man's place in the universe, it became hard to see how any particular idea of the moral life had precedence over any other. What could provide, beyond what we are and what we want to be, that further dimension of what we *ought* to be? Science could not do so, because it now examined causes, not ultimate purposes. Nor could anthropology, because all it revealed was the immense variety of pictures different societies have had of the good. The voice of God, which had hitherto given societies their most compelling ethical visions, had now been ruled *ultra vires*. And so, however conservative their intention, the ultimate effect of these philosophies was to weaken the idea of any moral authority beyond the self.

A fateful process had been set in motion. This was translated, in British philosophy, into a sharp distinction between facts and values; and in French existentialism into Sartre's declaration that human existence has no essence. Within three centuries, morality had moved from 'out there' to 'in here'. It had become a matter of individual will or preference or emotion or decision. To suppose that there were absolute moral standards which could be inferred from facts about revelation, the world or human nature was to have the wrong ideas about language or reason or human freedom.

Certainly moral philosophers could no longer tell us what to do; nobody could do that. At most they could clarify our choices and summon us to have the courage to make them.

This was bound, in the end, to have political implications. So long as moral values were seen to be 'out there' – in God or nature or society – it made sense to assume a strong relationship between morality and law. Law enforced objective values. But once the idea took hold that morality was a matter of individual choice, it became hard to see how it could be legislated. You might still talk about a moral consensus. But that hardly justified making illegal what a minority of the population sincerely believed was permissible. That would be what John Stuart Mill called the tyranny of the majority. Instead, so Mill argued, the only ground for making something illegal was that it caused harm to others. By the 1960s that case seemed irresistible, and as a result, in Britain and elsewhere, homosexuality and abortion were legalised. It takes a long time for the speculations of a philosophical avant garde to become the taken-for-granted commonplaces of ordinary life. But by now they have done so. The orthodoxies of our time are that morality is a private affair, a matter of personal choice, and that the state must be morally neutral.

THE ECLIPSE OF MORALITY

But this raises a fundamental question. Namely, does morality in any significant sense exist any more? Put this way, the question might seem absurd. After all we still use the language of morality. We speak of right and wrong, good and bad, justice and rights. But these are all words which were once thought to refer to objective principles, and it is just these that we now believe do not exist. The use of words like right and wrong suggests that there are impersonal standards by which our choices may be judged. But if there are no such standards, only choices, then moral language becomes an anomaly. Some recent writers have suggested just this: that our moral vocabulary is a vestige of an earlier age, and can no longer be used coherently.[7]

Perhaps the suggestion is not absurd. Pick up any contemporary book on how to live your life. It will begin by asking you to define your goals. It will teach you to organise your time and relationships to achieve them. You will learn assertiveness so as not to be inhibited by other people's agendas. Missing will be any suggestion of right and wrong. What is right will be what works for you. The great moralist of our time turned out to be Ernest Hemingway when he said, 'What is moral is what you feel good after and what is immoral is what you feel bad after.' In such an environment morality becomes a matter of technique alone: learning how to reach our objectives or achieve self- expression. We no longer talk of virtues but of values, and values are tapes we play on the Walkman of the mind: any tune we choose so long as it does not disturb others.

One of the great motifs of moral thought in the last century has been the crucial importance of private space, the territory in which we are simply free to be ourselves. Rarely in human history has the idea of an obligation imposed on us by others seemed so constricting and suffocating. And this has profound implications for our understanding of a whole range of issues. Marriage has become not a covenant but a contract without binding force beyond the consent of the partners. Families have moved toward more contractual relationships between parents and children. Sexuality is a matter of freely chosen lifestyle. Abortion is the right of a woman over her own body. Euthanasia is the right of each of us over our own lives.

What is missing in each of these cases is the idea once thought to be definitive of morality: that there can be obligations which constrain our choices, and duties that place a limit on desire. It is not that we have stopped thinking morally altogether. It is, rather, that our moral imagination is bounded by three central themes – autonomy, equality and rights – the values that allow each of us to be whatever we choose. The central character of our moral drama is no longer the saint or the hero, but the free self, unencumbered by attachments, unobligated by circumstance, freely negotiating its temporary contracts with others: Frank Sinatra singing, 'I did it my way.'

As a result, much of what we used to do as moral beings has come to seem repressive, even a denial of the human condition. To make moral judgements is to be judgemental. Calling a way of life wrong is an assault on the integrity or authenticity of others. The most fundamental of all parental wishes, to educate our children in our own morality, is indoctrination and a denial of their free development. We know that not all choices are wise. But we are reluctant to let that fact serve as the basis for a moral conclusion. Instead we make a distinction between acts and consequences. Acts are freely chosen; consequences are dealt with by the state. So governments are there to treat AIDS, child abuse, homelessness and addiction but not to disseminate a morality that might reduce them in the first place. Something quite revolutionary has happened to our ways of thinking: what I would call *the demoralisation of discourse*. We now no longer know what it is to identify a moral issue, as something distinct from personal preference on the one hand or technique on the other. We have arrived at Nietzsche's conviction that morality is no more than a camouflaged way of imposing our will on others.

Slowly and imperceptibly it has come to pass after all. The decline of religious ethics has brought about a metamorphosis of conscience into something which it is hard to call morality at all. If God does not exist, all *is* permitted. Or to put it less dramatically, religion and morality have moved in tandem. They have become privatised and lost their moorings in an objective order. We have reached Nietzsche's transvaluation of values. But what then happened to Nietzsche's nightmare? Why do we not feel ourselves straying as through an infinite nothing?

MORALITY AS LANGUAGE

But perhaps in some ways we do. Certainly we have lost our sense of being part of a single moral community in which very different people are brought together under a canopy of shared values. It has become difficult to see ourselves as part of a collective enterprise that preceded our birth, will persist after our death and which gives meaning to our struggles. Beyond producing and consuming, work and leisure, we find it hard to say what gives meaning to our lives. We have become inarticulate about the reasons for our choices. And the bonds between us, so important to understanding who we are, have become strained. We feel the need to liberate ourselves from our parents. We find it harder to imagine ourselves living on in our children. Each of our relationships, including marriage, has become provisional. The apartment we call the self has grown more self-contained, and therefore lonelier.

These changes have happened slowly and we have adjusted to them, which is why most of the time they are invisible. The greatest exile, as a Jewish mystic said, is not to know that you are in exile. But social commentators have given our situation a name. David Riesman called it 'The Lonely Crowd'; Peter Berger, 'The Homeless Mind'; Christopher Lasch, 'The Culture of Narcissism.'[8] Each of these phrases echoes the sense of being thrown in upon ourselves so that we can no longer hear that voice of the other that in morality was called altruism and in religion, transcendence. These voices are related, as religion and morality are related. For both have at their heart a search for an imperative reality outside the self. That is why both religion and morality have traditionally been understood as ways of seeing and hearing rather than of deciding.[9] The loss of these senses is one of the great privations of modernity.

We cannot go back to where we were. But neither are we condemned to stay where we are. We have reached the limits of individualism and we can now state its inner contradiction. Perhaps the best way of doing so is to think about language.[10] A baby expresses itself by crying; but until it learns a language it cannot tell us what it feels. We learn to speak by growing up among others who speak to us. Slowly and at first by imitation we acquire a language, until we are able to construct sentences by ourselves. In that process two things are essential. The first is the *community* of fellow speakers, our family and then an ever-widening circle. The second is the particular *tradition* embodied in the language itself, its meanings and associations, divisions and connections, each of which has a history we unconsciously adopt as we learn to become articulate. The greater our mastery of the language, the more we are able to say what we feel and imagine what we might become. Without community and tradition, there is no self-expression beyond the inarticulate cry of a child.

The history of moral thought since Spinoza has been a progressive eclipse of community and tradition. That was seen as a great liberation; but we can see it now as a great privation. Individualism condemns us to the task of constructing our own morality. But a private morality is no more possible than a private language. It is not surprising that in the twentieth century there have been philosophers, A. J. Ayer among them, who argued that moral talk was mere emotion. The word 'wrong' was an inarticulate cry masquerading as speech.[11] If so, far from reaching a state of sophistication, we have regressed to a moral childhood worse than that of which Spinoza and Freud accused religion. Moral education is not simply learning to make choices. It is becoming part of a community with a particular tradition, history and way of life. It is like learning a language. The contradiction at the heart of individualism is that there can be a self unencumbered by tradition, unfettered in its freedom. That is as inconceivable as an art without conventions or a thought without a language in which it can be expressed. The sovereign self, by dissolving its attachments, has become a kingdom without a country.

The Talmud tells the story of a man who came to the great sage, Hillel, and asked him to convert him to Judaism with one proviso: that he refused to accept rabbinic tradition. Hillel agreed and began by teaching him the Hebrew language. The next day he continued the lesson but this time changed everything he had taught him the previous day. The man protested. 'How can I learn if each day you teach me something different?' 'You see,' said Hillel. 'Even to learn a language you need to accept my authority as a teacher, and the traditions that give meanings to the words. How then can you learn Judaism without tradition and authority?'[12] That seems to me to be true of morality as well.

MORALITY AND COMMUNITY

The problem of our moral ecology is that we have thought exclusively in terms of two domains: the state as an instrument of legislation and control and the individual as the bearer of otherwise unlimited choices. But morality can no longer be predicated of the state, for we have become too diverse to allow a single morality to be legislated. Nor can it be located in the individual, for morality cannot be private in this way. We have neglected the third domain: that of community. But it is precisely as the member of a community that I learn a moral language, a vision and its way of life. I become articulate by acquiring a set of meanings not of my own invention, but part of a common heritage. I become connected to others through bonds of loyalty and obligation that are covenantal rather than contractual. And I become connected too, to the community's past and future, so that I can understand my life as a chapter in a larger narrative. That is what Jews, Christians and others do when they grow up within a religious tradition, and what Aristotle believed education was: induction into a community.[13]

Morality and religion turn out to be connected after all. It is not that we need to be religious to be moral, but that we need to be part of a community. And it was Emile Durkheim who argued that this was the heart of the religious enterprise, that it provided the symbols that constituted communities and thus made possible pursuit of the common good. Modernity has been deeply destructive of communities, and yet such persisting sense as we have of a good beyond ourselves is probably due to their influence upon us. Our religious traditions are an extraordinarily powerful moral resource. Not as a source of universal truth; for we live in a Babel of many truths.[14] But at the fundamental level of creating communities built on a moral vision, and in educating us to a collective pursuit of the good. Forming communities of meaning is religion's peculiar power. And it is in communities that the moral enterprise begins.

NOTES

1 Cited in Owen Chadwick, *The Secularisation of the European Mind in the Nineteenth Century*, Cambridge: Cambridge University Press, 1975, 10.

2 The quotation is from *La Gaia Scienza*.

3 I should add that I do not consider this paragraph a remotely adequate view of religious ethics. It does, however, roughly summarise the popular view of the biblical tradition, which came under attack from Spinoza onwards. Medieval religious ethics, in Judaism, Christianity and Islam, developed a high degree of philosophical sophistication, a fact which subsequent philosophical critiques have rarely fully addressed.

4   Again it should be noted that these objections are easily countered. Judaism, for example, distinguished between two kinds of moral code, the Mosaic and the Noahide commands. The former were specific to the covenant between God and the Jewish people; the latter represented a kind of universal law binding on mankind as such. Nor did it consider obedience out of fear of punishment or expectation of reward the highest kind of motivation. To the contrary: this was obedience 'not for its own sake,' or service of God out of fear rather than love. Maimonides defines the lover of God as one for whom reward and punishment are incidental, and who 'performs the truth because it is the truth.'

5   Lionel Trilling, *Sincerity and Authenticity*, Cambridge, Mass.: Harvard University Press, 24.

6   Spinoza, *A Theologico-Political Treatise*, translated by R.H.M. Elwes, New York: Dover, 1951, 76.

7   This, for example, is the burden of Alasdair MacIntyre's argument in his *After Virtue*, London: Duckworth, 1981. MacIntyre's thesis is that 'we possess indeed simulacra of morality, we continue to use many of the key expressions. But we have – very largely, if not entirely – lost our comprehension, both theoretical and practical, of morality.' The case had been argued earlier by Elizabeth Anscombe.

8   David Riesman, Nathan Glazer and Reuel Denney, *The Lonely Crowd*, New York: Doubleday, 1954; Peter Berger, Brigitte Berger and Hansfried Kellner, *The Homeless Mind*, Harmondsworth: Penguin, 1974; Christopher Lasch, *The Culture of Narcissism*, New York: Norton, 1978.

9   See Iris Murdoch, *The Sovereignty of Good*, London: Routledge, 1970.

10 For a similar exposition, see Stuart Hampshire, *Morality and Conflict*, Oxford: Blackwell, 1983, 140–169.

11 This theory, which subsequently became known as *emotivism*, was contained in chapter 6 of A. J. Ayer's *Language, Truth and Logic*.

12 Babylonian Talmud, *Shabbat* 31a.

13 See, for example, M. F. Burnyeat, 'Aristotle on Learning to be Good,' in Amélie Oksenberg Rorty (ed.), *Essays on Aris-*

totle's Ethics, Berkeley: University of California Press, 1980, 69–92.

14 I am not denying here that there are universal moral truths. I believe there are. They are represented in Judaism by the idea of the Noahide commands (on this, see David Novak, *The Image of the Non-Jew in Judaism,* New York: Edwin Mellen Press, 1983 and his *Jewish-Christian Dialogue*, New York: Oxford University Press, 1989) and in Christianity by Aquinas' concept of natural law. But these amount to less than a substantive and comprehensive moral code. They are a kind of minimum threshold rather than a Platonic essence of morality. Stuart Hampshire put it well when he wrote that 'human nature, conceived in terms of common human needs and capacities, always underdetermines a way of life' (*Morality and Conflict*, 155).

3

THE FRAGILE FAMILY

Philosophers love posing dilemmas. Here is one. You are standing in the National Gallery at the opening of an art exhibition. Suddenly a fire breaks out and spreads with enormous speed. In front of you is a priceless Leonardo. To your right is one of the country's most respected elder statesmen. To your left is your four-year-old daughter. You can only rescue one of them. Which do you save?

Well, if you emerged into the open air with the painting or the statesman you might have contributed to the greater good. But I wonder whether we would altogether trust you as a human being.

Somehow the family goes to the heart of our sense of moral obligation. Our ties to our children and to our parents are fundamental; and not as the result of any rule or reflection. Rather, they have to do with who we are and our peculiar relationship with those who brought us into the world and those we've brought into being in turn. We would be inclined to say they are an instinct, a natural feeling. But they are also a matter of culture, of acquired values.

In 1976 there was an earthquake in Communist China. The Chinese press carried a report about a man who had rescued a local Communist officer from a fallen building. His own child was also trapped, and he had heard him crying for help.

But he chose instead to save the officer, whose social value he considered to be greater. By the time he returned to the wreckage for his son, he found him dead. The Communist newspapers wrote about the incident as an example of proper behaviour.[1]

What these examples suggest is that there is more than one way of ordering our loyalties. We might inhabit a culture in which family ties mattered less to us than they do now. But what they might also suggest is that such a culture would be an altogether colder and less personal one. The family is not just one of our social institutions, but in a very real sense, the one on which all others depend. Our families might change, but if they did, much else would change in the way we understood the world, and not necessarily for the better.

But that, of course, is precisely what has been happening. Throughout Europe and America in recent years, changes in the family have been significant and sudden. In Britain, for example, the latest estimates are that 37 per cent of marriages will end in divorce. One in four children is born outside of marriage.[2] Cohabitation prior to or in place of marriage has increased to the extent that it is soon likely to be the norm. The proportion of single parent families has risen, from 8 per cent in 1971 to 14 per cent in 1987. In some urban areas the figure is much higher. In inner London, for example, it is more than one in four.[3]

Not only that. More people are staying single for longer. There are more, and more open, homosexual and lesbian relationships. So that we have moved, within the space of two decades, from the convention of the stable nuclear family – husband, wife and children in permanent relationship – to an extraordinary diversity of sexual and social arrangements, many of which are consciously temporary and provisional. One projection suggests that by the end of the century only one child in two will have parents who were married when it was born and who stay together until it has grown up.[4]

FROM TRADITION TO CHOICE

Some would argue that these changes are more apparent than real. People are what they always were. It is just that what they once did secretly they now do openly. Until the 1960s, there were established conventions of sexuality and marriage, and some of them were given the force of law. Since then homosexuality has been legalised, divorce made easier, and illegitimacy has had most of its legal disabilities removed. But there

is no reason to suppose that until then what people did always conformed to what they were supposed officially to do.

Peter Laslett, for example, has calculated that even in the nineteenth century – that age of high moral rhetoric – three out of every five first children were extramaritally conceived.[5] As for divorce, the rising figures are at least in part the result of legal reforms which have made available to everyone what had been in the past the preserve of the few. Besides which, divorce is not necessarily a weakening of the institution of marriage. It may be a sign that we expect more from it. The present situation, then, may simply be one in which the choices people always sought are now neither legally foreclosed nor morally condemned. It is not so much that behaviour has changed, as that we have stopped imposing on it the straitjacket of myth, morality and law.

But this, I think, is simply mistaken. A way of life is not only constituted by what people do, but also by the framework in which they understand what they do. Removing the legal and moral sting from cohabitation, divorce, illegitimacy and homosexuality does not leave the world unchanged. The gradual transformation by which sin becomes immorality, immorality becomes deviance, deviance becomes choice, and all choice becomes legitimate, is a profound redrawing of our moral landscape, and alters the way we see the alternatives available to us.

The change has been revolutionary. Think how far we are from the world of Jane Austen's heroines, where demure young ladies spent their time anxiously waiting for the right man – in terms of class, income and character – to come along. It is harder still for us to think ourselves into the Jewish townships of Eastern Europe only three generations ago, made famous by *Fiddler on the Roof*. There, in the world of my grandparents, a couple would simply not meet without elaborate enquiries and negotiations taking place beforehand between the respective families, often with the help of that archetypal Jewish figure, the matchmaker. Boy and girl met with a view to marriage, and who could marry whom was governed by an elaborate social code, never made explicit but understood by everyone. Was Chaim the tailor a suitable match for Mendel the grocer's daughter? The whole town would have a view on the matter, so it was as well to get it right. The couple might eventually meet and be left alone, but the community was, in a sense, there in the room with them.

Since then, a whole cluster of associations has been exploded. In the nineteenth century society was still deeply divided by class, religion and ethnicity, and this set firm limits on whom you could think of marrying. Today those demarcations have almost gone. Not only that. Birth control has separated sex from having children. The entry of the state into education and welfare has, to some extent, separated having children from raising them. The waning of religious teachings has removed the stigma of cohabitation and illegitimacy, and marriage itself has lost its once sacramental character. Living together and the ease of divorce have taken from our most basic relationships the sense of permanence with which they were once invested. Old lines of connection and separation have disappeared, leaving us in a world without boundaries.

It is therefore not surprising that novelists, playwrights and film-makers have taken boy meets girl as the primal scene of the breakdown of tradition. Because it is here that the breakdown has been most immediate and dramatic. Even in that ordered world of Jane Austen, for example, we can hardly fail to notice the new importance the novelist gives to the individual and his or her private emotions. That long journey of modernity, from society to self, has already begun. And it was not long before English novelists were exploring a new kind of emotion, romantic love, which for the first time had the power to break through the iron boundaries of class. By 1908 the Jewish writer Israel Zangwill had produced a play, *The Melting Pot*, in which a Jewish boy whose parents had been killed in the Kishinev pogrom meets and marries the daughter of the Russian colonel who had been responsible for the murder. Marriage within the faith, which had been until now a central religious value, was dismissed as antiquated prejudice.

As the century proceeded, even romantic love began to seem an anachronism. Sexuality declared its independence from marriage: better bed than wed. The very idea of moral rules began to seem out of place in the context of personal relationship. Where once, only a few generations ago, individuals met and in that meeting carried with them the internalised history of a community, today we meet as spontaneous selves in a present which bears few marks of a shared past or a predictable future. It is not then simply that what we once did secretly we now do openly. Rather, the values that underlie what we do have been radically transformed.

CRITICS OF THE FAMILY

But have these been changes for the better? In some respects surely they have. There can sometimes steal upon us a mood of misty nostalgia in which the sun always shines on the past. But in the case of the British family that involves selective vision. It overlooks a history of often loveless but interminable marriages, and the dependent and subordinate position of women. In Hogarth's engravings of the eighteenth century, and Dickens' novels of the nineteenth, there are scenes of appalling brutalities practised on children. Some theorists have suggested that it was only with the decline in infant mortality rates, at the end of the eighteenth century, that parents could take the risk of investing affection in their children. It was only when you were sure your child would live that you could afford to give it love.[6] And it took enlightened social thought in the nineteenth century to end the employment of seven-year-olds in the cotton mills of Lancashire. The move from the authoritarian to the democratic family, in which each of the members has a say; the idea of love as the basis on which two people come together and get married; even the importance of the family itself a 'haven in a heartless world' are all relatively recent, and enrich our sense of relationship. So it is hard to place all the changes in the modern family on the side of loss.

But there have been at least some voices to suggest that we have not gone far enough. One influential line of modern thought has argued that the family is in need not of change but abolition. Karl Marx suggested that the bourgeois family lay at the heart of the capitalist economy. Radical post-Freudians argued that it was a source of psychological distress, schizophrenia especially. Feminists like Shulamith Firestone saw it as the perpetuation of patriarchy. Sir Edmund Leach, in a famous sentence in his Reith Lectures, summed it up when he said that 'Far from being the basis of the good society, the family, with its narrow privacy and tawdry secrets, is the source of all discontents.'[7]

Now whether or not we agree with these ideological critics, they take us to the heart of the proposition with which I began, namely that the family is not just one of our institutions, but a formative one, the crucible in which much else of our social structure takes shape. We learned from Malinowski's studies of Melanesia and Margaret Mead's of Samoa that there are very different ways of organising sexuality, kinship and socialisation. But we also know that these would result in different attitudes to politics, property, and the relationship between the individual and society. The French anthropologist Emmanuel Todd has recently traced an impressive set of connections between different family systems and the worldwide distribution of political ideologies. The absolute nuclear family, for example, is closely related to liberal democracies, and authority in the home to authority in the state.[8] The family is the birthplace of our social world. So we might arrange our families differently. But it will be a different kind of world that we will be creating.

It was C. H. Cooley who pointed out that the deep sentiments we call human nature are formed by the primary groups in which we are raised. 'If these are essentially changed,' he said, 'human nature will change with them.'[9] It was a discovery that the pioneers of the kibbutz made early on. Having abolished marriage and the family and handed children over to collective child-minders, they found that they had raised a generation quite unlike themselves: less emotional, striving and individualistic; more matter of fact and inclined to think of identity in terms not of the self but the group.[10] As our families fragment, so do the deepest structures of our consciousness. When a certain kind of family breaks down, so do the values which once linked parents and children and gave continuity and character to our inherited world.

This is precisely why ideological radicals have focused on the family. Change it and you change humanity. But let us turn the argument round. If changing the family would change the world, might not protecting the family be the best way of protecting our world? This is, I believe, what religious tradition has been doing until now.

THE BIBLICAL FAMILY

The Hebrew Bible is above all a book about the family. It begins with one: Adam and Eve and the command to bring the next generation into being. And from then the book of Genesis never relaxes its grip on the subject. It endlessly turns to some new variation in the relationship between husbands and wives, parents and children. Abraham and Sarah, Isaac and Rebekkah, Jacob, Rachel and Leah: these are not miracle workers or agents of salvation. The heroes and heroines of Genesis are simply people living out their lives in the presence of God and the context of their families.

This is not accidental to the thrust of the biblical narrative. Rather, it forms the foundation of the Bible's larger moral and social themes. The family is, firstly, the matrix of individuality. It is that enclosed space in which we work out, in relation to stable sources of affection, a highly differentiated sense of who we are. It is hard to imagine a culture which didn't possess a close family structure arriving at the breathtaking idea that the human individual is cast in the image of God.

De Tocqueville once wrote that 'as long as family feeling is kept alive, the opponent of oppression is never alone.' By which he meant that the family is the great protection of the individual against the state. It is no coincidence that totalitarian regimes have often attacked the family. Against this, it was the Bible that gave rise to the great prophets who dared to criticise kings. The family is the birthplace of liberty.

Not only that. It is where we care for dependents, the very young and the very old, those to whom we gave birth or who gave birth to us. It is a short step from this to the biblical vision of society as an extended family, in which the poor and powerless make a claim upon us, by virtue not of abstract principle but of feelings of kinship. It is this that lies behind the prophetic identification with the widow, the orphan and the stranger. They are not merely people with theoretical rights. They are part of the family.

Marriage, for the Bible, is a covenant and one closely related to that which joins humanity to God and the members of society to one another. A covenant is not merely a contract. It is a religious, not just a legal agreement. It is one in which the partners bind themselves to mutual fidelity and concern. So that the biblical idea of society, which flows from its view of marriage, is different from the secular idea of a social contract. It is not just an association for mutual advantage. It is a covenant of loyalty and trust.

More fundamentally still, the family is where we discover our past. The Bible instructs us to teach our children diligently, speaking of God's law when we are at home or on the way, when we lie down and when we rise up. Repeatedly it tells parents to tell children the story of their origins, the exodus and the long journey to freedom. The family is where traditions are handed on, where I learn that the past lives on in me, and through me in my children. It is the basis of collective memory. On it rests the biblical view of history as the stage on which the covenant between man and God is enacted and within which we construct a just society. The family is 'a narrative institution,'[11] the place where we tell the story of where we came from. Its breakdown leads to what J. H. Plumb called 'the death of the past', the loss in our society of a historical sense.

So that the family as a religious institution is what holds much of our moral world in place. It lies behind our ideas of individual dignity and freedom, of social kinship and concern, and our sense of continuity between the future and the past. Lose it and we will lose much else as well.

A RELIGIOUS INSTITUTION

Why then do we seem to have been doing just that? Because of one of the most powerful legacies of the Enlightenment, our idea of the abstract individual, detached from the collective bonds of history and sentiment. The self of modern moral theory has no limits on what it can choose to do or be, other than those externally set by law. No one way of life has any intrinsic precedence over any other so long as it is freely chosen.

Such a theory, I argued in the previous chapter, ultimately dissolves morality. But certainly it deconstructs the family. It robs it of its ethical foundations. At every stage the concept of the family stands counter to the idea of unrestricted choice. To be a child is to accept the authority of parents one did not choose. To be a husband or wife is to accept the exclusion of other sexual relationships. To be a parent is to accept responsibility for a future that I may not live to see. Families only exist on the basis of choices renounced. And our secular culture has made that voluntary closure of options hard to accept or even understand.

The family has persisted as an institution, but increasingly we have lacked the resources to say why it should. Our intellectual world has not given it space. To the contrary, our current lack of any norms relating to sexuality and marriage precisely reflects the supreme importance we have given to the abstract individual, without binding commitment either to the past or to the long-term future, open-endedly free to choose or unchoose any style of life. The family has lost its moral base.

Admittedly, this has not happened because of Enlightenment philosophy alone. It has happened because of social changes of which that thought was an early anticipation. Education and welfare, which once took place within the family, have been largely transferred to the state. Television means that information is no longer filtered to the child primarily through its parents. The pace of change means that we can no longer assume a common world with our children. And in a technological society, age loses the authority of wisdom. It is our children who understand computers, not us. The mass entry of women into the work force has dramatically changed our child-rearing practices. These changes, along with the breakdown of our moral traditions, have weakened the force of family bonds. We cannot unwrite them. But we cannot suppose that they do not have momentous implications for those who will inherit the world we have made.

The irony of the 1980s is that the decade which witnessed the worldwide retreat of the state before the individual, also witnessed the accelerated disintegration of the family, the primary protection of the individual against the state. Our private lives will be significantly eroded if one child in two will no longer reach maturity in stable association with the people who brought it into being. What then will stand between us and the impersonal operations of the free market and the state? From whom, other than our parents, will we learn who we uniquely are? The twentieth century, through Freud and others, has taught us the enduring influence of our early experience of childhood. But the twentieth century has rendered the family uniquely problematic. And the world that witnesses its loss will be a colder and less human place.

But it is here that we come up against a surprising fact that has run like a connecting thread through these lectures. Despite the many factors making for its erosion, the family persists. It still lies at the heart of our sensibilities. Few things so distress us as television pictures of children separated from their parents, or move us like scenes of families being reunited. Overwhelmingly we do still marry, and hope that our marriages will last. In a recent survey almost nine out of ten of those interviewed said that they valued faithfulness as the most important ingredient in marriage. We still believe in the family, without quite knowing why.

The family is a religious institution that survives in a secular culture. Our attachment to it makes no sense in terms of the theories or social changes that have surrounded us since the Enlightenment. But it makes a great deal of sense in terms of the argument I have been advancing, that we are still more religious than we suppose. Faith is not measured by acts of worship alone. It exists in the relationships we create and it lies deep in our moral commitments.

The Jewish tradition saw the family as the greatest religious domain of all. The first command in the Bible is to have children, and there is no act we can perform that testifies more lucidly to faith in the future of our world. The survival of the Jewish people through almost four thousand years of exiles and dispersion is due, above all, to the strength of its families. And it was when parents and children sat together round the table, that they could most immediately feel the touch of the Divine presence.

The family is a much assaulted, much wounded institution, but it endures: testimony to a sense of covenantal love that can still break through the secular surface of our lives and surprise us by its unexpected and religious strength.

NOTES

1 The example is taken from Michael Wyschogrod, *The Body of Faith*, Minneapolis: Seabury Press, 215–216.
2 In 1989, the figure was 27 per cent. *The Times*, 20 September 1990.
3 The figures are taken from Kathleen Kiernan and Malcolm Wicks, *Family Change and Future Policy*, London: Family Policy Studies Centre, 1990.
4 Ibid., 43.
5 Quoted in Ferdinand Mount, *The Subversive Family*, London: Jonathan Cape, 1982, 253.

6   Philip Aries, *Centuries of Childhood*, New York: Knopf, 1962.

7   E. R. Leach, *A Runaway World*, London, 1968, 44.

8   *Emmanuel Todd, The Explanation of Ideology: Family Structures and Social Systems, Oxford: Blackwell, 1988.*

9   Quoted in Ronald Fletcher, *The Shaking of the Foundations: Family and Society*, London: Routledge, 1988, 30.

10 Bruno Bettelheim, *The Children of the Dream*, London: Paladin, 1971.

11 Lionel Trilling, *Sincerity and Authenticity*, Cambridge, Mass.: Harvard University Press, 1978, 139.

4

PARADOXES OF PLURALISM

Earlier this year, Harold Pinter delivered a public lecture entitled *Is Nothing Sacred?*[1] It had been written, not by Pinter, but by Salman Rushdie who for security reasons was unable to deliver it himself. Here was one of those charged moments in which we felt the inescapable clash of two cultures: modernity and tradition in the shape of an iconoclastic novelist and an outraged Islam. At stake was not only the rarified issue of blasphemy, but even the most fundamental question of what words mean, and what a book is. Throughout the controversy Rushdie had argued that *The Satanic Verses* was, after all, just a novel, in which words are intended neither to cohere with reality nor to represent the views of their author. Muslims, raised in a tradition of sacred texts, saw the written word as altogether more freighted with significance: a sentence is an entity in its own right and an author cannot escape responsibility merely by invoking the conventions of the modern novel. Who was right? There was, of course, no answer. Not because the question was difficult but because the two cultures that addressed it excluded one another.

In his lecture, Rushdie spoke directly to the theme of the novel in contemporary society. It was, he said, a privileged arena; born, in Carlos Fuentes' words, 'from the fact that we do not understand one another, because unitary, orthodox language has broken down. ' He went on to tell this parable.

Imagine that you are imprisoned in a large, rambling house. It is full of strangers and friends. At some point you realise that there is no way out. Then one day you discover a room full of voices, talking about the house and everything and everyone in it. You find solace in this room; without it you would go mad. That, said Rushdie, was the function of the novel. 'Literature is the one place in any society where, within the secrecy of our own heads, we can hear voices talking about everything in every possible way.'

It was a provocative definition, both of literature and of sanity. Because we might well reply that listening to voices talking about everything in every possible way is not sanity but the quickest route to madness, and that it is precisely the condition not just of high literature but of the whole of our fragmented culture. For sanity, the inhabitants of Rushdie's house might well gather together, first just a few, then in growing numbers, to listen to someone who could tell them the story of the house and why they came to be there, and what lies outside, though no one has ever returned. This religious narrative might seem to them the one thing that made living in the house tolerable. And when one day their gathering was interrupted by a stranger with a radio from which poured voices talking about everything in every possible way, they might feel that some privileged arena had been intruded on. The two parables, like the two cultures, exclude one another. And conflict of this kind is buried like an explosive charge in one of the great underexamined words of our culture: the word *pluralism*.

ASSIMILATION AND THE IDEA OF A PUBLIC CULTURE

What is a plural society and how did we arrive at it? It's worth remembering that not long ago the phrase might have seemed a contradiction in terms. In 1959, Lord Devlin argued that 'What makes a society of any sort is community of ideas, not only political ideas but also ideas about the way its members should behave and govern their lives.' He added, 'If men and women try to create a society in which there is no fundamental agreement about good and evil they will fail.'[2] He was, of course, speaking about morals rather than culture. But there is little doubt that he had in mind a relatively unified society, shaped not only by moral teaching but by a broad set of common traditions, what Hegel called *Sittlichkeit*: the shared symbols and civilities that made England so quintessentially English.

It was an elevated view of this culture that, for example, inspired John Reith in the early days of the BBC. Reith believed that broadcasting had a responsibility to reflect and strengthen what he called 'that spirit of common sense Christian ethics which we believe to be a necessary component of citizenship and culture.' The voices speaking on John Reith's BBC might talk about everything, but not in every possible way. They were recognisably speakers of a common language, members of a cultural establishment. In fact, as late as 1955, when a Mrs Margaret Knight delivered a radio talk suggesting that there could be morality without religion, one daily newspaper complained that the BBC had allowed 'a fanatic to go on the rampage beating up Christianity' and one of the governors of the BBC asked whether the broadcast constituted seditious libel.

It was this shared culture that underlay the liberalism of the nineteenth century. During that century civil rights were extended to Catholics, members of the Free Church and Jews, and a clear distinction was made between the public and the private domain. Religious confession became a matter of private conscience; and access to the universities, professions and public office was open to all. But there remained a distinctive language of society, and whoever wished to enter had to learn it. Irishmen, Jews and other new arrivals had to pass through what John Murray Cuddihy called the 'ordeal of civility'[3] and acquire the accents, nuances and intricate codes of polite society. One of the rules was that religious non-conformity was permitted so long as it was private, and Jews learned to hide their identity so well that Sidney Morgenbesser once defined their creed as *incognito ergo sum*.

The key word in this process was assimilation. As new arrivals entered still traditional societies, they were expected to dissolve from groups into individuals and absorb the dominant culture. By any earlier standards this was a benign procedure. Before the nineteenth century, religious and ethnic minorities had been barred from at least some civil rights. But it was not without its traumas, particularly for the transitional generation. The Jews of Central Europe felt them acutely.[4] Having broken away from their parents' faith, they found themselves still regarded as outsiders in the new society whose manners they'd so carefully cultivated. They were in that psychologically devastating no man's land between an excluded past and an excluding present; so that an observer like Jacob Klatzkin, writing in the early twentieth century, could speak of a whole generation of 'rent and broken human beings ... diseased by ambivalence, consumed by contradictions, and spent by restless inner conflict.'[5] It was the intellectuals of transition, double outsiders, who helped shape the modern mind: among them Marx, Durkheim, Freud, and Kafka. Salman Rushdie is, I suppose, their Islamic counterpart.

Assimilation was painful. But it seemed to be the only way a society could sustain its coherence while admitting large numbers of newcomers. It was in America in the early twentieth century that a quite different idea began to take shape. By then, vast numbers of immigrants had entered the United States, too many and too varied to suppose that they would rapidly merge into the melting pot. It was in 1915 that a young philosopher called Horace Kallen proposed a new model of a culturally diverse society. He made a clear distinction between the state and what today we would call ethnicity. And he regarded it as a misconception that each new immigrant group should undergo assimilation to the dominant culture. Instead he envisaged that while there would be a 'common language' of America, each group 'would have for its emotional and involuntary life its own peculiar dialect or speech, its own individual and inevitable aesthetic and intellectual forms.'[6] It was the first argument for cultural pluralism. What Kallen saw was that liberalism would have to move one stage further. It had emancipated minorities as private citizens, but it had not yet made space for them as public cultures. The next step was inevitable. America should become cosmopolitan.[7]

CONFLICT AND FRAGMENTATION

That was pluralism in theory. In practice, though, it was not until the 1960s that a whole series of developments in America and Western Europe shattered the idea of a single public culture. It was then that the civil rights movement in the States announced that black was beautiful. Local identities began to be asserted: Welsh and Scottish nationalism among them. There were large new immigrant communities in Britain. There was talk of resurgent ethnicity. Nathan Glazer and Daniel Moynihan stated bluntly that the point about the melting pot is that it didn't happen.[8] Grandchildren of immigrants developed a fascination for lost family traditions. Marcus Hansen propounded the law that the third generation labours to remember what the second generation strove to forget.[9] The secular city had rediscovered what Harold Isaacs called 'the idols of the tribe.'

And it was not only ethnicity that began to tear at society's seamless robe. There was the youth rebellion against moral conformity. There were communes and countercultures and alternative lifestyles. And for once the guardians of the older order had no reply. The idea of a strong national culture had, after all, served as the foundation of the century's greatest evils, fascism and communism. The past seemed to have used up its moral capital. The future was best left in the hands of those who would inherit it. Theologians spoke about the death of God and the shaking of the foundations. Liberals argued successfully that law could not be used to enforce private morality.[10] And with remarkable speed that set of fundamental agreements which Lord Devlin spoke of as the basis of society had been dissolved. The lines between private and public were redrawn. Political opinions, which were once not discussed at dinner, were now emblazoned on tee shirts. Sexual language and imagery which had been sheltered behind a code of reticence now became publicly sayable and showable. It had not been long before that George Bernard Shaw had shocked theatre audiences by his use, in *Pygmalion*, of the word 'bloody'. We had become restless with the Victorian ordeal of civility: being one thing in public and another in private. Within a decade society had taken on the character of Salman Rushdie's definition of literature: voices talking about everything in every possible way. Pluralism was liberalism carried through to the public domain.

But in the process, there is a dramatic change in our social ecology. Precisely because liberalism gained power in the nineteenth century it was able to take for granted a high degree of shared morality and belief, without having to reflect too carefully on the institutions that sustained it. Pluralism takes much further the idea that there is no such shared basis of society. Public policy should be neutral in matters of religion and morality and should merely adjudicate impartially between conflicting claims. The problem is that pluralism gives rise to deep and intractable conflicts while at the same time undermining the principles by which they might be resolved. It disintegrates our concept of the common good.

Sometimes we can witness this fragmentation at an early stage. Take, for example, the recent argument over religious broadcasting. It produced an unusual convergence of interests. Evangelicals and at least some secularists would both prefer a situation in which religious groups were able to buy time to deliver their message, if necessary on minority interest channels. To both sides the move from broadcasting to narrowcasting, from a wide to a specialised audience, represented a clear gain. To the secularists it would free mass audience channels from having to provide religious programmes. To the religious, evangelising on the air would mean not having to hold back from proclaiming the truth as one sees it. Both sides gain and no one, apparently, loses. But there is a loser. It is the idea of a shared culture at a level beyond entertainment and information.

Anyone who has ever delivered a religious broadcast knows how difficult it is to speak to an unknown and open audience. To our fellow believers we can address words of fire; to a wider public only the vaguest generalities. Broadcasting as opposed to narrowcasting is low on authenticity. But if we are to have a public culture, and one with a religious dimension, it is a discipline we have to undergo. We have to learn to speak to those we do not hope to convert, but with whom we wish to live. Narrowcasting frees us from that burden. But it moves us nearer a situation in which opinion is ghettoised into segmented audiences, and where the increase of choice means that we only have to listen to voices with which we agree.

There are more serious examples. Take the one with which I began. Liberals and religious minorities have both objected to a situation in which only Christianity is protected by the blasphemy laws. Instead, all major faiths should have equal protection. But how? One side argues that the blasphemy laws should be extended to cover them all. But that way conflict lies, because Christianity, Judaism and Islam have all at some stage been regarded as blasphemous by one another. Buddhists, for their part, opposed the proposal because their own rejection of monotheism might be construed as blasphemous by Christians, Muslims and Jews alike. Perhaps blasphemy could be translated from an offence against religion to an assault on deeply held convictions. But if so, it is difficult to see why religious convictions should be especially privileged; and if all convictions were given equal weight, we would rapidly move to a situation where the beliefs of any might constrain the expressions of all. Liberals have therefore argued for an abolition of the offence of blasphemy altogether. But this would give equal protection to each religion by giving no protection to any.[11]

Or consider the problem of religious education. For liberals, the answer seemed to lie in teaching all children all faiths. The problem is that giving many religions equal weight is not supportive of each but instead tends rapidly to relativise them all.[12] It produces a strange hybrid in which the primary value is personal choice, and we feel free to choose bits of one tradition and place them alongside pieces of another, disregarding the different ways of life that gave them meaning in the first place. A multicultural mind can use Zen for inwardness, Hassidic tales for humour, liberation theology for politics, and nature mysticism for environmental concern. But that is a little like gluing together slices of da Vinci, Rembrandt, Van Gogh and Picasso and declaring the result a composite of the best in western art. The simultaneous presence of voices talking about everything in every possible way, degenerates rapidly into mere noise.

Parents might well conclude that the only way of passing on their values to their children was to choose a highly segregated education. And that surely was pluralism's promise: that different religious and ethnic traditions could defend themselves against assimilation, in this case assimilation into multiculturalism itself. The demand for segregated, denominational schools grows rather than diminishes in a pluralist society. But this offends against another principle of pluralism, namely, the harmonious mix of different groups. As a result, the Commission for Racial Equality has recently argued for the end of all denominational schooling: a proposal to which all religious groups will be equally opposed.[13]

FIRST AND SECOND LANGUAGES

These are conflicts in which pluralism comes down firmly on both sides at once. The reason is that at its heart are two incompatible views of a plural culture. One sees it as a place where many traditions meet and merge. The other sees it as an environment where distinct traditions can guard their separate integrity. At stake are two conflicting views of freedom, one which focuses on the individual, another which emphasises the group. Each side sees the other as a profound threat to its values. Liberals see religions as an assault on personal autonomy. Traditionalists see liberals as undermining religious authority. In both cases, non-negotiable values are at stake. Pluralism becomes a moral bank account that is always overdrawn. It endorses mutually exclusive visions of the good, and by abandoning the concept of a common good, leaves us inarticulate in the face of cultural collision.

From this deadlock, there *is* a way out, and that is to think of a plural society not as one in which there is a Babel of conflicting languages, but rather as one in which we each have to be bilingual. There is a first and public language of citizenship which we have to learn if we are to live together. And there is a variety of second languages which connect us to our local framework of relationships: to family and group and the traditions that underlie them.[14] If we are to achieve integration without assimilation, it is important to give each of these languages its due.

Our second languages are cultivated in the context of families and communities, our intermediaries between the individual and the state.[15] They are where we learn who we are; where we develop sentiments of belonging and obligation; where our lives acquire substantive depth. Pluralism should not simply be neutral between values. Rather, it must recognise the very specific value of Christians, Muslims, Buddhists, Sikhs, Hindus and Jews growing up in their respective heritages. Traditions are part of our moral ecology, and they should be conserved, not dissolved, by education.

But this is only viable if we develop an equally strong first language of common citizenship, and it must have a richer vocabulary than the single word 'rights'. It was Horace Kallen himself, the first advocate of pluralism, who argued the need for values which everyone must agree on 'if they mean to live freely and peacefully together as equals, none penalising the other for his otherness and all insuring each the equal protection of the law.'

Our language of citizenship has a history. It belongs to what Felix Frankfurter described as 'the binding tie of cohesive sentiment' that underlies the 'continuity of treasured common life' of a nation. But like all languages, it evolves. And we must respect both the history and the evolution. Perhaps we would no longer say as confidently as John Reith that the 'spirit of common sense Christian ethics' is a 'necessary component of citizenship and culture.' But that tradition remains a significant part of our national life, even if it has been joined by other voices, some religious, some secular.

We have tended to neglect that first language in recent years. We would be hard pressed to say what shared values today made us a society. Perhaps in this age of Europeanism and domestic diversity, we have moved beyond the whole idea of a national identity: our attachments are either larger or smaller than that. It may be only at times of conflict, like the Falklands war, or for that matter the World Cup, that we are strongly aware of national belonging at all.

If so, I believe it is a mistake. The more plural a society we become, the more we need to reflect on what holds us together. If we have only our second language, the language of the group, we have no resource for understanding why none of our several aspirations can be met in full and why we must restrain ourselves to leave space for other groups. We begin to have expectations that cannot possibly be fulfilled. This creates sectarian leadership, the politics of protest, single issue lobbies, and sometimes acts of violence. Pluralism can lead to a contemporary tribalism and no-one has painted a darker picture of it than Tom Wolfe in his novel. *The Bonfire of the Vanities*. In its pages contemporary New York has become a society of conflicting ghettoes, white Anglo-Saxon Protestant, black, Irish Catholic and Jewish, and to wander out of your own into someone else's is to fall headlong into nightmare. That surely, we must avoid.

The task of representing shared values traditionally fell, in England, to the established Church. Our current diversity makes many people, outside the Church and within, feel uneasy with that institution.[16] But disestablishment would be a significant retreat from the notion that we share any values and beliefs at all. And that would be a path to more, not fewer, tensions. In a society of plurality and change, there may be no detailed moral consensus that can be engraved on tablets of stone. But there can and must be a continuing conversation, joined by as many voices as possible, on what makes our society a collective enterprise: a community that embraces many communities.

Keeping this first language alive means significant restraints on all sides. For Christians, it involves allowing other voices to share in the conversation. For people of other faiths it means coming to terms with a national culture. For secularists, it means acknowledging the force of commitments that must, to them, seem irrational. For everyone, it means settling for less than we would seek if everyone were like us, and searching for more than our merely sectional interests: in short, for the common good.

We do not need to look far for a metaphor of our situation. The book of Genesis gives us our first description of what Salman Rushdie calls the breakdown of language, the confusion of voices talking about everything in every possible way. But the Tower of Babel is not the end of the biblical narrative, merely its beginning. In the next chapter, Abram is called to a faith that will not become the faith of everyone, merely the covenant of a single extended family. Other peoples will testify to God in their own distinctive ways. In a plural world, there are many paths to the Divine presence, many languages in which faith is expressed. What then is the religious imperative after Babel? Simply this. That Abram is told: in you will all the families of earth be blessed.[17] That necessary tension between second and first languages, being faithful to one tradition and yet a blessing to others, is one of the great themes of the Bible. As it deserves to be, of our time.

NOTES

1   Salman Rushdie, *Is Nothing Sacred?*, The Herbert Read Memorial Lecture, Cambridge: Granta, 1990.

2   Patrick Devlin, *The Enforcement of Morals*, Oxford: Oxford University Press, 1983, 9–10.

3   John Murray Cuddihy, *The Ordeal of Civility*, Boston: Beacon Press, 1987.

4   For one impressive study of the effects of this process, see Sander L. Gilman, *Jewish Self-Hatred*, Baltimore: Johns Hopkins University Press, 1986.

5   Jacob Klatzkin, 'The Galut is Unworthy of Survival,' in Arthur Hertzberg (ed.), *The Zionist Idea*, New York, Atheneum, 1981, 323.

6 Horace M. Kallen, *Culture and Democracy in the United States*, New York, 1924, 124.

7 For a survey of Kallen's ideas, see Sidney Ratner, 'Horace M. Kallen and Cultural Pluralism,' *Modern Judaism* 4:2 (May 1984), 185–200.

8 Nathan Glazer and Daniel P. Moynihan, *Beyond the Melting Pot*, Cambridge, Mass.: MIT Press, 1970.

9 Marcus Lee Hansen, *The Problem of the Third Generation Immigrant*, Augusta Historical Society, Rock Island, 1ll., 1938. See Will Herberg, *Protestant-Catholic-Jew*, New York: Anchor, 1960.

10 The classic text was H. L. A. Hart, *Law, Liberty and Morality*, Oxford: Oxford University Press, 1963.

11 See *Law, Blasphemy and the Multi-Faith Society*, London: Commission for Racial Equality, 1990.

12 It was for this reason, among others, that the British Muslim community was opposed to the multi-faith approach of the Swann Report [*Education for All: The Report of the Committee of Enquiry into the Education of Children from Ethnic Minority Groups*, HMSO, 1985]. See Mervyn Hiskett, *Schooling for British Muslims*, London: Social Affairs Unit, 1989; S.J.D. Green, 'Beyond the Satanic Verses,' *Encounter* 74:5 (June 1990), 12–20.

13 Schools of Faith: Religious Schools in a Multicultural Society, *London: Commission for Racial Equality, 1990.*

14 On first and second languages, see Robert Bellah, Richard Madsen, William Sullivan, Ann Swidler and Steven Tipton, *Habits of the Heart*, London: Hutchinson, 1988.

15 See Peter L. Berger and Richard John Neuhaus, *To Empower People*, Washington: American Enterprise Institute for Public Policy Research, 1977; Charles Murray, 'In Pursuit of Happiness,' *Dialogue* 87 (1990), 41–47.

16 See Stewart Lamont, *Church and State: Uneasy Alliances*, London: Bodley Head, 1989.

17 Genesis 12:3.

5

FUNDAMENTALISM

For some reason, religious conviction in the modern world produces in us a mixture of surprise, fascination and fright, as if a dinosaur had lumbered into life and stumbled uninvited into a cocktail party. I remember, three years ago, taking part in a panel on the use of bad language in broadcasting. Everyone else addressed the subject of obscenity. I was asked to speak about blasphemy. No one had given blasphemy much thought for many years. The one exception – Mary Whitehouse's prosecution of *Gay News* – seemed to be just that: a stray pebble tossed into a sea of calm indifference.

At the time I quoted T. S. Eliot who believed that blasphemy was no longer possible.[1] He thought that you can only blaspheme if you profoundly believe in the reality of that which you profane. No one, according to Eliot, believed that strongly any more. Along with faith, blasphemy too had died.

Everyone agreed, and the subject sank without trace. Few of us could have imagined that within a few months *The Satanic Verses* would make blasphemy front page news throughout the world and that eighteen people would die in religious protests about a novel. Here was religious belief very much alive in the way the Bible had once portrayed the presence of God: a whirlwind shattering rocks and uprooting the cedars of Lebanon, fascinating in its power, terrifying in its destructiveness. It was the hurricane our weather forecasters failed to predict. Why did the resurgence of religion take us by surprise? And how shall we react to it? We lamented the loss of faith. Shall we fear its rediscovery still more?

One picture dominated our understanding of religion in the modern world. Faith was being ousted from one room after another of its once stately home. Science investigated nature, history explored the past, businesses maximised profits, technology increased control and governments mediated conflicts, all outside the sacred canopy of faith. Religions might still be true, but they had lost what Peter Berger called their plausibility structure, their objective embodiment in society.[2] Faith might remain a private consolation, but it could hardly govern the public domain.

The priest, guardian of the sacred, was left stranded: the last amateur in a world of professionals, the last practitioner of the unquantifiable. For healing, we would prefer a doctor; for catharsis, a psychotherapist. Welfare and education had been transferred to the state. And prayer had become what one churchman recently described as a list of ultimatums given to God when all other avenues had been exhausted. The human imagination would still need the narratives that explained ourselves to ourselves. But art and drama long ago declared their independence from religion. Our domestic parables and metaphysical myths are no longer told in religious texts. Instead they are played out on the screen as soap opera and science fiction. Wherever the man of God turned, he found someone else already doing his job. Religion was the ineffable become the unemployable.

The most perceptive theorists of secularisation were well aware that none of this meant that the great religions were about to be eclipsed. But it meant that some hard bargaining would have to take place. Faith no longer had its mansion. Could it negotiate for itself at least a modest apartment in the tower of Babel? And if so, which of its now cumbersome furniture would it have to throw away?

So began the varied strategies of religious liberalism and neoorthodoxy. Religion would concede the loss of its empire. It would grant independence to the vast domains of knowledge and decision where once it had been the colonial power. But it would reserve some restricted territory for itself: as a mode of experience, or the voice of conscience, or a spring to social action, or as some immediate, self-contained, even mystical way of knowing. The very powerlessness of religion might be its salvation. In Hamlet's words, it could be bounded in a nut-shell and still count itself king of infinite space.

Nowhere were these issues addressed more searchingly than in Protestantism, by figures like Schleiermacher, Bultmann and Bonhoeffer. But throughout the nineteenth and twentieth centuries Judaism followed the same trajectory, as the sudden move from ghetto to Enlightenment strained the bonds of rabbinic tradition. Catholicism and Islam, too, had their modernist voices, who stressed the need for reinterpretation of doctrine and religious law.

We can hardly understand religious reactions to modernity without appreciating the extent to which scientific rationalism seemed to carry all before it. From Hume and Voltaire onward, religious belief became a subject of ridicule and disdain. It was primitive, irrational, an opiate, a neurosis, an illusion for those who could not face reality. What John Murray Cuddihy wrote about Jews could be applied to believers of many other kinds: that before they could enter the modern world they had to learn a 'consciousness of underdevelopment.'[3] For Christians, the challenge was intellectual. It came from biblical criticism, Darwin and the relativising of belief. For Muslims it tended to be social and political: European colonial rule and the sense that Islam had been overtaken by the West. Some form of accommodation seemed necessary: the only way to recover self-respect. Modernity had won the battle, and religion had to salvage what it could from defeat.

THE RETURN OF RELIGIOUS CONSERVATISM

That was the picture. The intellectual, social and political changes required by a modern economy meant the loss of that stable world in which alone religious faith could grow. Here and there, there might be groups still untouched by the process – rural communities, the American Bible belt, the Jewish townships of Poland and Russia. Some might even opt out of it altogether, like the Hassidim, the Jewish mystical circles of Eastern Europe. But that meant strict withdrawal, enclosed communities and a sectarian form of religious organisation. There might be occasional revivals, as there were in Victorian Britain and periodically in America. But these were no more than lingering pools left by the outgoing tide. Churches and synagogues had either to make their peace with secular values, as they did in America, or lose adherents, as they did in England. Either way, religion had lost its power to shape societies. It had become the sacred facade of an increasingly secular social order. By the close of the nineteenth century Oscar Wilde was already calling religion the fashionable substitute for belief. Preachers were left to lament the 'melancholy, long withdrawing roar' of the retreating sea of faith.[4]

Pictures govern our expectations. The image of inexorable secularisation made any large-scale resurgence of religious fervour improbable. Even the unexpected appearance among students in the 1960s of mysticisms, cults and counter-cultural movements was no more than a minor parenthesis in the larger proposition.

But it was just then that observers began to detect something else. In 1965 Charles Liebman published an article on 'Orthodoxy in American Jewish Life.'[5] Until then, it had been assumed that Jewish Orthodoxy was in a state of terminal decline. As Jews arrived in America, they set foot on the escalator of acculturation and left their religious baggage behind. The second and third generations joined progressively more liberal congregations, if they identified religiously at all. Now for the first time, Liebman's article drew a different picture. Far from being ready to expire, Orthodoxy was 'the only remaining vestige of Jewish passion in America' and 'the only group which today contains within it a strength and will to live that may yet nourish all the Jewish world.'

A few years later, Dean Kelley produced a strikingly parallel analysis of American Christianity.[6] Documenting the growth and decline of various denominations, he found that those that were prospering were groups like the Southern Baptists, Pentacostalists, Seventh Day Adventists, Jehovah's Witnesses and the Mormons. What they had in common was that they rejected the accommodations of the mainline churches. They were absolutist, highly disciplined and zealous to proselytise. They demanded and evoked strong commitment. They provided clear answers to moral and metaphysical questions. The evidence since then confirms Liebman's and Kelley's analysis. The more liberal, accommodationist organisations have declined. Conservative and evangelical movements have continued to grow.

It seemed as if a large-scale cultural conversion was taking shape, a turning of the tide. Secularised Christians were being born again. Assimilated Jews were taking the path of religious return. A more considered analysis showed that this was not quite so. Those who crossed denominational boundaries were highly visible but numerically few. A society-wide revival was not in the making. The millennium was not yet in sight. But what *was* happening was significant nonetheless. Those whose faith was most demanding had larger families and gave their children a strong religious education. They had low rates of attrition and were effectively raising a new generation who shared their values. Against the denominational drift, they were holding their own, and demography was in their favour. In an open society, the strongest religious commitments were those best fitted to survive.

This gave confidence to once demoralised traditional voices. In the backlash against the chaos of the 1960s, their convictions rang out clearly. They knew what they believed, and their opinions had none of the complicating subordinate clauses of the religious liberals. They spoke with that rarest of modern accents: authority. They had learned the lessons of modern communication and organisation. Conservative and evangelical groups became the most enthusiastic users of radio, television and mass mailing. In America, the 'Moral Majority' became a significant force of political pressure. And from these long neglected circles came the unmistakable sounds of success. By the end of the 1970s, they could claim that they had now acquired the influence long yielded by liberals. It was a matter less of numbers than of mood. But it was a significant turn, and raised serious questions about the picture of religion in the modern world. Modernism, liberalism and rationalism no longer looked invincible. Going with the secular flow had ceased to be the best strategy.

MODERNITY AND ITS DISCONTENTS

Why did it happen? We can speak only in the broadest of terms, but we can surely say this. Our image of religion these past two centuries has been part of a larger picture. It is reflected in the key words that came to dominate social thought in the nineteenth century: civilisation, progress, evolution, even the word 'modern' itself as a term of praise.[7] These words testify to the profound future-orientation of modern culture. The new is an improvement on the old. Optimism and anti-traditionalism go hand in hand.

It was a compelling scenario. Science would fathom the mysteries of nature, and technology would harvest its treasures. Reason would replace superstition, and tolerance would triumph over prejudice. The modern state would bring participation and equality. The individual would have liberty of choice, freed from paternalist authority. So long as modernity delivered its promises, the voices of lamentation could be ignored.

But at some stage in the 1960s, profound doubts began to be expressed. Technology had given us the power to destroy life on earth. Economic growth was consuming the environment. The modern state had the power to organise tyranny and violence on a scale hitherto unknown. Racial animosities had not disappeared: they had fired the ovens of Auschwitz. No utopia had yet been brought by revolution, and the free market was increasing inequalities between rich and poor. In the secular city there was homelessness and violence, and individualism had made the most basic relationships vulnerable. Robert Bellah caught the mood when he said: 'Progress, modernity's master idea, seems less compelling when it appears that it may be progress into the abyss.'[8]

No-one was so well prepared for these doubts as those long disattended conservative religious leaders. They had developed a deep pessimism about modern culture. They had preached against its excesses and idolatries. And now they could say: We told you so. They spoke directly to modern discontents. Against the fragmentation of knowledge they could offer wholeness of vision. Against an over-reaching civilisation they spoke a coherent language of restraint. Marx and Freud had called religion an illusion. But now religion could reply that it had rejected the greatest illusion of modern times: the self-perfectibility of man. Precisely those religious movements that seemed to have been left behind by modernity became, ironically, an avant garde of post-modernity.

But it is just here that we must confront our ambivalence. We lamented the loss of faith. Shall we fear its rediscovery still more? One word expresses that ambivalence: fundamentalism. It is fundamentalism, or what is sometimes described as religious extremism or fanaticism, that makes us wonder whether religious revival might be not a refreshing breeze but a destructive hurricane.

DIMENSIONS OF FUNDAMENTALISM

What is fundamentalism? The term itself is unhelpful, because it yokes together different faiths, phenomena and contexts as if they were all one thing. But it does at least help us to focus on the problems of a premodern faith in a postmodern world.

The word was coined in America in the 1920s in the wake of a series of pamphlets setting out the fundamentals of Christian belief.[9] And at its simplest level it is just that – a kind of common-sense defence of Orthodoxy in a highly secular age, a reaction against what is seen as a liberal intelligentsia's subversion of established beliefs. What makes this a peculiarly twentieth century phenomenon is that our culture has moved so far from its religious roots that it now takes almost an act of defiance to use words like revelation, truth and authority in their traditional sense. A fundamentalist refuses to let faith be relativised by history or science or sociology. Revelation stands above time and speaks to us now as clearly as it ever did. We may have changed wavelengths on our cultural radio, but we can still hear the voice of God.

But fundamentalism is not simply another name for Orthodoxy. In Protestantism, for example, it is the belief not only that Scripture is true in every respect, but also that for the most part it is to be understood literally.[10] A fundamentalist tends to reject not only secularism and liberal theology, but also the kind of Orthodoxy – often called neo-Orthodoxy

– which believes that serious consideration must be taken of the intellectual environment of faith. Neo-Orthodoxy – represented by figures like Karl Barth in Christianity and Samson Raphael Hirsch in Judaism – maintains that religious doctrine, though true and timeless, needs always to be interpreted in the light of our particular time. That, to the fundamentalist, sounds like sophistry. Instead religious texts speak to us now, directly and without interpretation, because nothing significant has changed between the moment of revelation and modern times.

Thus far fundamentalism is an approach to religious belief. But now a problem arises. To hold traditional beliefs is one thing. To do so in a deeply secular culture is another. How do you live your faith in a world that daily seems to ignore it? Broadly speaking, there are two alternatives. One is to disengage as far as possible from society, the other is to try and change it. Orthodox Jews tended to do the first: to live in enclosed communities. But other conservative religious groups favoured the second. This has meant, especially in America, campaigns to reverse permissive legislation on abortion, homosexuality, pornography and other perceived symptoms of moral decline. It is when fundamentalism moves from a defence of doctrine into the political arena that we begin to fear a war of cultures. It is one thing to believe in absolute truth; something else to seek to legislate it in a plural culture. At this point fundamentalism crashes headlong into liberal politics, and the stakes of the confrontation are high.

But fundamentalism can go deeper still. Many religious believers experienced modernity not as a process to be endured but as an assault to be resisted.[11] It seemed as if their most precious beliefs were being ridiculed by an intellectual é lite, as if the foundations of the world were being removed. For Christians, it came in the form of secularity; for Jews, assimilation; for Muslims, westernisation. And it is here that fundamentalism offers a theory, not of doctrine or culture but of history. Seen through sacred texts, present conflicts can become cosmic drama, rich in images of apocalypse: the holy war against the infidel, the global confrontation before the end of days, the pursuit of the imminent millennium. And once we have reached this point, fundamentalism can, in certain circumstances, move from spiritual vision to extremism and ultimately violence.

It is when it meets and merges with nationalism that we risk a terrifying return to the wars of religion. It is no accident that the most intractable conflicts of recent years – Northern Ireland, the wars and massacres of the Middle East, even the emerging rivalries of Eastern Europe – have had a religious dimension. In an age when secular ideologies have lost their power, revolutionary leaders have enlisted religious passion instead. It is an explosive combination. War becomes a holy struggle against the demonic other. Terror is sanctified. Hatred becomes a form of piety. The present moment is charged with metaphysical meaning, brushing lesser considerations aside. The complexities of conflict are resolved into a simple dualism of light against darkness. A savage catharsis will bring the promised age.

TOLERANCE: SECULAR OR RELIGIOUS?

For the past two centuries we have assumed that religion, if it survived at all, would do so at the margins of society. This allowed us to leave unresolved the great question of religious coexistence. As Reinhold Niebuhr pointed out, religions create communities of love within their own boundaries, but they find relationships across the boundaries far more problematic.[12] The three great monotheisms in particular – Judaism, Christianity and Islam – are absolute in their claims of truth, and therefore tend to divide the world into believers and unbelievers. Historically this could lead, within nations, to a denial of rights to other confessions and, between nations, to holy war.

Perhaps it was Judaism's historical good fortune to be deprived of political power at an early stage. Jews were used to living as a minority in exile. And this led rabbinic tradition[13] to articulate an important series of doctrines: that Judaism is not an exclusive path to salvation,[14] that cultures that respected the rule of law could not be considered idolatrous,[15] and that 'the ways of peace' must equalise the rights of all faiths.[16] The best tutor in religious tolerance is a situation in which you cannot survive without it. As a result Jews were religiously predisposed to welcome a liberal political order. In 1783, on the threshold of Enlightenment, Moses Mendelssohn could point out that since the destruction of the second Temple seventeen centuries earlier, Judaism had lacked any connection between religion and state.[17]

Within Christianity too, it was the gradual separation of religion and state that allowed, in the seventeenth and eighteenth centuries, a doctrine of universal rights to emerge. Even so, religious prejudice could persist in secular forms. By the late nineteenth century, throughout central and eastern Europe, Christian anti-Judaism had become racial antisemitism. It took the Holocaust to make us realise that there is no nightmare like hatred harnessed to the absolute state.

Islam's encounter with modernity took a somewhat different course. In many countries it came as a religious and political onslaught: the impact of western ideas on a proud and ancient civilisation. It was not easy to integrate the two. At first, cultural accommodation seemed possible, but the new values were radically subversive of the old. The new world turned out to be less a liberation than a humiliation. So that throwing off the recent past could encompass nationalism and religious revival at the same time. The very reintegration of religion and state could seem like a return to authenticity: away from the decadent secularism of the West to the lost harmonies of a golden age.[18] The power of Islamic fundamentalism in the late twentieth century has taken us by surprise. But we recall that it was only a century ago that the development of empire and the spread of Christianity were seen as going hand in hand. It takes a great catharsis to make us recognise that other religions than our own possess integrity and rights.

Our assumption that religion would always be marginal in modern societies led us to believe that human rights could rest on a secular foundation. The intolerances of religion would be resolved by the simple fact that they would lack power. That was a fatal error in the nineteenth century; still more so today. None of us now inhabits a space occupied only by fellow believers. We are at constant risk of being implicated in events far from home. Innocent shoppers or passengers on a plane are blasted out of existence by a bomb planted in a cause on which they never took sides. The effects of nuclear or chemical war are unrestricted by national borders. The remote has become terribly near. And our understanding of international economics and the environment completes the thought that nuclear weapons began: that no man, no country and no religion is an island in this interconnected world.

Fundamentalism is the belief that timeless religious texts can be translated directly into the time-bound human situation, as if nothing significant has changed. But something *has* changed: our capacity for destruction and the risk that conflict will harm the innocent. So long as tolerance and respect for human rights rest on a secular foundation they will be overridden by those who believe they are obeying a higher law. And the fact that the great universal monotheisms have not yet formally endorsed a plural world is the still unexorcised darkness at the heart of our religious situation.[19]

We may see, in the future, more national identities expressed in religious terms, as secularism loses its persuasive power. And the challenge of peace in the 1990s may well be one to which only religious leaders can rise. Behind us lies a bloodstained history of inquisitions, crusades and jihads. But beyond that lies Genesis' momentous disclosure that every human being – the unredeemed, the infidel, the other – is still the image of God. Toleration is not, as G. K. Chesterton said, 'the virtue of people who do not believe anything.' It is the virtue of those who believe unconditionally that rights attach to the individual as God's creation, regardless of the route he or she chooses to salvation. That is counter-fundamentalism, the belief that God has given us many universes of faith but only one world in which to live together. It is a truth to which we now have no alternative.

NOTES

1   T. S. Eliot, *After Strange Gods*, New York, 1934.

2   Peter L. Berger, *The Sacred Canopy*, New York: Doubleday, 1967.

3   John Murray Cuddihy, *The Ordeal of Civility*, Boston: Beacon Press, 1987, 167.

4   The words are from Matthew Arnold's poem, *Dover Beach*.

5   Charles Liebman, 'Orthodoxy in American Jewish Life,' in Morris Fine and Milton Himmelfarb (eds.), *American Jewish Year Book*, vol. 66, New York: American Jewish Committee, 1965, 21–92; reprinted in Reuven Bulka (ed.), *Dimensions of Orthodox Judaism*, New York: Ktav, 1983, 33–105.

6   Dean Kelley, *Why Conservative Churches are Growing*, New York: Harper and Row, 1972. See also Dean Kelley, 'Why Conservative Churches are still Growing,' *Journal for the Scientific Study of Religion* 17, 165–172; Reginald Bibby, 'Why Conservative Churches *Really* Are Growing: Kelley Revisited,' *Journal for the Scientific Study of Religion* 17, 129–137.

7   Raymond Williams, *Keywords: A Vocabulary of Culture and Society*, London: Flamingo, 1983.

8   Robert Bellah, Richard Madsen, William Sullivan, Ann Swidler and Steven Tipton, *Habits of the Heart*, London: Hutchinson, 1988, 277.

9   See E. Sandeen, *The Roots of Fundamentalism*, Chicago: University of Chicago Press, 1970; George M. Marsden, *Fundamentalism and American Culture*, New York: Oxford University Press, 1980.

10 See James Barr, *Fundamentalism*, London: SCM, 1977, and *Escaping from Fundamentalism*, London: SCM, 1984.

11 To be sure, fundamentalist groups of various kinds are among the most enthusiastic users of modern communications and political techniques. But a distinction must be made between the instrumental *use* and the intellectual *acceptance* of modernity. Equally, as many observers have noted, the political involvement of fundamentalist groups invariably involves a measure of accommodation and secularisation. This is a central paradox of fundamentalism as a religious movement in a secular age.

12 Reinhold Niebuhr, *Moral Man and Immoral Society*, New York: Charles Scribner's, 1947.

13 These ideas were implicit in biblical Judaism, in the tension between the ideas of universal monotheism and a particular covenantal people; but they were given formal expression in the rabbinic literature.

14 Tosefta, *Sanhedrin* 13:1; Maimonides, *Mishneh Torah, Melakhim* 8:11.

15 See Jacob Katz, *Exclusiveness and Tolerance*, Oxford: Oxford University Press, 1961.

16 See Talmudic Encyclopaedia, *Darkhei Shalom*, vol. 7, 716–724.

17 Moses Mendelssohn, *Jerusalem*, translated by Allan Arkush, Brandeis University Press, 1983.

18 See, for example, Imam Khomeini, *Islam and Revolution*, translated by Hamid Algar, London: KPI, 1985.

19 I realise that this is a strong statement, but it is deeply felt. Great advances have been made in Christian-Jewish relations in recent decades. The Vatican declaration, *Nostra Aetate*, in 1965 was one example. The 1988 Lambeth resolution on 'The Way of Dialogue' was another. Christian theologians, among them Paul van Buren, A. Roy Eckardt and Rosemary Radford Reuther, have wrestled, with enormous courage, with the issues. As a Jew, I can only express my admiration and awe at the soul-searching that has taken place within Christianity after the Holocaust.

But questions remain, above all those of 'supercessionist' theology and the Church's mission to the Jews. For recent Jewish perceptions of the state of dialogue, see Geoffrey Wigoder, *Jewish-Christian Relations since the Second World War*, Manchester: Manchester University Press, 1988, and Marc Saperstein, *Moments of Crisis in Jewish-Christian Relations*, London: SCM, 1989. For an important collection of responses to religious pluralism, see John Hick and Paul Knitter (eds.), *The Myth of Christian Uniqueness*, London: SCM, 1987, and for a Jewish response to dialogue, see David Novak, *Jewish-Christian Dialogue: A Jewish Justification*, New York: Oxford University Press, 1989.

My own understanding of religious truth is that it is covenantal, and that one covenant does not exclude another. See Jonathan Sacks, 'The Interfaith Imperative,' *Christian-Jewish Relations* 23:1 (Summer 1990), 5–14; and, for a Christian statement of a similar position, Paul van Buren, 'Covenantal Pluralism?' *Common Ground* 1990, 3, 21–27. For a sensitive philosophical exploration of religious particularism, see Michael Wyschogrod, *The Body of Faith*, Minneapolis: Seabury Press, 1983.

6

A COMMUNITY OF COMMUNITIES

'Religions,' Bryan Wilson once said, 'are always dying.'[1] He might have added: but they never quite seem to die. Faith confounds prediction. One of our most tenacious beliefs these past two centuries has been that modern society would be the stage of religion's final last performance. Against that I have suggested another phenomenon: the surprising persistence of faith.

It has been an unlikely and by no means simple story. Let us take an example. A hundred years ago we could have walked through the Jewish communities of London and seen a process in the making. We would begin in the East End, in Whitechapel. And we would find ourselves deep in the atmosphere of Eastern Europe. It is here that the Jewish immigrants arrived in the wake of the Russian pogroms of the 1880s. It is overcrowded, bustling, noisy, poor: an ethnic ghetto full of strange accents and smells. There are Jewish businesses everywhere: tailors and bootmakers and every few hundred yards a little synagogue. There is no doubt that we are in Jewish London.

A few miles to the West, in the synagogue in Duke's Place, we would find an altogether different kind of community: Jews who had been in England long enough to have established themselves economically, and to some extent socially as

96

well. They have combined their religious Orthodoxy with a decidedly Victorian manner. The men wear top hats and frock coats; the synagogue is decorous and ornate; the sermon will quote Shakespeare rather than the Talmud and will be delivered in grandiloquent prose. Anglo-Jews, conscious of the novelty of emancipation, have taken great pains to become anglicised.

Some have gone further still. Continuing our walk, we would arrive at London's first Reform synagogue, whose members believe that substantial accommodations are needed if Jews are to become part of English society. To the scandal of the Orthodox, they have introduced a mixed choir and an organ, abridged some of the festivals and amended the prayer book to make it more congenial to a rationalist age. A journey of five miles on a single morning in 1890 would have taken us through three generations in the process from immigration to acculturation.

Something like this journey has been the fate not just of Jews but of most of us, from English villagers to Irish Catholics to the most recent Sikh and Hindu immigrants. It is less a change of place than a change of consciousness: from parochial to cosmopolitan, local community to open society, from tradition to modernity. On the way, all the old ties are weakened: accents and attachments, particular identities, above all, religious commitment. They belong back in the foreign country called the past, accessible now only through nostalgia. Or so it seemed.

Because, suspending our hindsight and knowing only what we have seen in 1890, we could write the future of those Victorian Jews. In the journey from the East End to the West, there has been a slow attenuation of Jewishness, from a total environment to occasional synagogue attendance. Jews were preparing for the twentieth century by leaving their ancient world behind. We might have predicted that by 1990 they would have assimilated to the point of invisibility. There would be, at most, a few pockets of resistance: Jews who turned their back on the modern world. But for the rest, an open society would do what generations of persecution could not achieve. It would put faith into the museum of antiquities. The four generation rule seemed unbreakable. The grandfather prays in Hebrew. The father prays in English. The son no longer prays. The grandson is no longer Jewish.

THE RECOVERY OF RELIGIOUS IDENTITY

That was the prediction: secularisation among Christians, assimilation among Jews. For a long time the evidence supported it. But now it needs to be revised. Already in 1957, the American sociologist Nathan Glazer noted that something momentous had happened to Jews; more precisely, something had not happened. They had not stopped being Jews.[2] By 1990 we can speak not merely of survival but of revival. In Anglo- as in American Jewry, every year there are new synagogues and schools. Jews are rediscovering the traditions whose loss their grandparents lamented. At Oxford today there are courses in Yiddish, the very language immigrant Jews laboured to forget. The study of Jewish history flourishes as Jews relive their once- relinquished past. *Back to the Future* has replaced *Gone with the Wind*.

And not only among Jews. Because this recovery of identity has been widespread, most obviously among ethnic groups, but in evangelical revivals as well. We will each explain it our own way. For Jews, the story will include the transfiguring events of the Holocaust and the birth of the state of Israel. For Christians it might be told in terms of the traumas of modernity: fears of nuclear and chemical warfare, ecological concerns and the ever-growing inequalities between rich and poor. For Muslims it might speak of disillusionment with the

West and hopes for a cultural and political renaissance of Islam. Other groups will explain in other ways how ethnicity persisted or new forms of community were found.

It is as if we have reached the limits of assimilation into the neutral space of secular society. And hitting them, we have rebounded back. A plural culture almost forces us into identifications of this kind. As national identity grows weaker, other identities fill the vacated space, and of these religion is the most personal and transmissible. Not only among minorities. Perhaps the most unexpected fact about contemporary Britain is that the overwhelming majority of the population has not stopped being Christian. It may not be reflected in church-going or religious observance. But it answers the question increasingly unanswerable in other terms. The question: Who am I?

But the prediction was not altogether mistaken. What has become clear, if paradoxical, is that religious identity can go hand in hand with a decline along all measurable axes of religious behaviour. We practise the rituals of faith less often. We go to places of worship rarely. We can be, it seems, religious and secular at the same time. And religion in a secular society is not what it is in a religious society.

Take contemporary Jewry. Like every other group, it has been affected by new patterns of behaviour radically at odds with traditional norms: mixed marriage, for example, or homosexuality or the rejection of sexually differentiated roles. In the past, Jews who were drawn to these behaviours would have known that in so doing, they were parting company with Judaism. Today they are more likely to seek a home for them in the synagogue itself. So that liberal Judaism is driven to ever wider acceptance of untraditional values. It survives by becoming secularised.

But this creates an opposite reaction too. Jewish survival depends in high measure on the strength of the family: on the decision of Jews to marry, create Jewish homes and raise children committed to continuing the covenant. Until recently, that could almost be taken for granted. But no longer. There has been a sharp rise, in the last two decades, in the rates of mixed marriage, non-marriage and divorce. It has become harder to hand the tradition on across the generations. So that Jews who place a high value on family and continuity feel bound to raise the barriers between themselves and the surrounding society. They survive by refusing to become secularised.

So religion in a secular society is polarised. For a majority it is a tenuous association that does not break the rhythms of a life whose pulse is elsewhere. For a minority, it has become a counter-revolution against an apparent slide into moral anarchy. A plural and fragmented culture translates its divisions into the religious domain. It encourages both an extreme and diffuse liberalism and an extreme and concentrated conservatism, each obeying a different religious imperative: the one to bring religion to where people are; the other to bring people to where religion has always been.

Each religion has had its own critical issues: birth control or abortion or sexual ethics, the ordination of women or the interpretation of doctrine; in the case of Judaism, the very question, Who is a Jew? Whether we speak of post-Vatican II Catholicism, or the current Church of England or diaspora Jewry, the coalition between liberals and conservatives has become increasingly fragile. Where one side speaks of autonomy, equality and rights, the other speaks of tradition, obedience and authority. They have become, as Shaw once said, divided by a common language.

BEYOND THE INDIVIDUAL

But this is just part of a wider disintegration brought about by the loss of what Peter Berger called 'the sacred canopy',[3] that overarching framework of shared meanings that once shaped individuals into a society. In its place has come pluralism: the idea that society is a neutral arena of private choices where every vision of the good carries its own credentials of authenticity. But pluralism carries an explosive charge of conflicting interpretations. We have seen some of them in recent arguments about blasphemy, religious broadcasting, multi-faith education and denominational schools. The irony of pluralism is that it leads us to expect a growth of tolerance, while in fact it lays the ground for new forms of intolerance. By dismantling and privatising the concept of a common good it means that no one position is forced to come to terms with the reality of any other.

It is no accident that as pluralism has gained ground, there has been a sharp increase in racial tension and anti-semitism, and an air of insolubility about our most basic moral disagreements. Once we lose a common language, we enter the public domain as competing interest groups rather than as joint architects of a shared society. Communities are replaced by segregated congregations of the like-minded. This is an environment that encourages mutually exclusive visions of the good. At its extreme it produces a clash of fundamentalisms, some liberal, some conservative, neither with the resources to understand the other.

It was Robert Bellah who suggested that our social ecology is no less important, and perhaps more fragile, than our natural ecology. It is damaged, he said, not only by war, genocide and political repression, but also by 'the destruction of the subtle ties that bind human beings to one another, leaving them frightened and alone.'[4] That is a penetrating description of our own atomised culture. We have neglected the institutions needed to sustain communities of memory and character. The assumption has been that society could exist on the basis of the private choices of individuals and the occasional intervention of the state, as if these were the only significant entities in our social landscape. But a plural society needs a moral and cultural base. Ideally, to use Martin Marty's phrase,[5] it is a community of communities: a series of environments in which we learn local languages of identity alongside a public language of collective aspiration. It requires two things. It needs communities where individuals can feel that their values are protected and can be handed on to their children. And it needs an overarching sense of national community in which different groups are participants in a shared pursuit of the common good.

In recent years the key word in our political vocabulary has been the *individual*. In the 1960s the state retreated from the legislation of morality. In the 1980s it drew back from the economy and welfare. It was assumed in both cases that public responsibility would be replaced by private virtue. Marriage and the sanctity of life would remain as values but would no longer be legally enforced. We would still be pained by deprivation, but we would address it through self-help and philanthropy. Private virtue was the building that would stay standing once the scaffolding of the state was removed.

But without the communities that sustain it, there is no such thing as private virtue. Instead, there is individualism: the self as chooser and consumer. And the free market can be a very harsh place for those who make the wrong choices. The shift from state to individual at a time when our communities have eroded has carried a high cost in poverty, homelessness, broken families and the drugs, vandalism and violence that go with the breakdown of meaning. In an individualistic culture, prizes are not evenly distributed. They go to those with supportive relationships: to those, in particular, with strong families and communities.

Think back again to the Jewish immigrants of the 1890s. They were not, I suspect, exceptional individuals. But they came with one great asset: a still influential religious tradition. Few groups have moved faster from inner city to suburbia. It is not hard to see why. In part, it had to do with the value Jews always placed on the family and education. Parents invested their hopes in their children and made sacrifices for their schooling. In part it had to do with community. Jews had had a long tradition of creating voluntary organisations, their own networks of support. And in part too it had to do with religious self-definition. The Jewish garment workers in the East End had other sources of self-esteem than their place in the economic order. They had a history. They could stand outside their social situation. They could say, with Rabbi Adin Steinsaltz, that this is the worst of all possible worlds in which there is still hope. It was those essentially religious structures of solidarity that broke through the cycle of deprivation. It is hard to see how that dynamic could have been created by the state on the one hand or disconnected individuals on the other.

RELIGION AND COMMUNITY

Community is the missing third term in our social ecology: the *local* communities where we discover identity, and the *national* community where we conduct our conversation about the common good. At both levels, there is an important religious dimension. Locally, our many faiths and denominations are often our first source of belonging. It is in our congregations and ethnic communities, intermediate between the individual and the state, that we find our sense of enduring value, of continuity through change. It is here that the individual is rescued from isolation, that identities are forged and traditions handed on. The critic Peter Fuller once wrote that he doubted whether art could ever thrive 'outside that sort of living, symbolic order, with deep tendrils in communal life, which it seems a flourishing religion alone can provide.'[6] That is true about morality and the family as well. Their natural environment is community, and creating communities is religion's special power. It is this realm, larger than the individual, smaller than the state, that is in our time the primary religious domain.

But religion has a larger role to play as well, in charting our shared moral landscape, that sense of a common good that we need if our communities are to cohere as a society. In Britain, as in America, it was the biblical tradition, in dialogue with secular voices, that throughout the nineteenth and early twentieth centuries tempered competition with compassion, individualism with responsibility, and gave the search for social justice its prophetic voice. It allowed us to understand ourselves not as replaceable units of production and consumption but as unique individuals capable of enduring commitments of benevolence and love.

So long as that tradition was influential, we could count ourselves part of a continuing narrative handed on between parents and children, a drama of redemption or salvation within which our moral judgements took on a massive solidity. We stood in collective worship before the great mystery of existence itself, knowing that neither we nor our time were the measure of all things. It was this that led Alexis de Tocqueville, writing about America in the 1830s, to call religion the first of its political institutions, that which taught Americans the 'art of being free.' He saw that individualism needed a counterbalance if it was not to consume the very society which gave it birth. Our political structures need a moral base which they cannot themselves create but without which they cannot survive. A culture split between economic and moral individualism and a series of sectarian minorities is unlikely to remain cohesive for long.

We have undervalued religion as part of our ecology. It is not hard to see why. With the rise of science we no longer needed it to explain our world. The growth of the modern state relieved it of its roles in welfare and education. Nor did we need religion as a form of social control, when we had law in the public domain and unrestricted choice in our private lives. Religion might survive. Whatever else happened, human beings would still be mortal and would suffer. They would respond to epiphanies and consolations. But if faith survived, it would do so in the margins of life. It would occupy a role in our culture not unlike that of music or art, a fascination for some, but for most an occasional indulgence. As a public presence, its time had passed. It had died, but most people were too polite to say so.

The obituary was stunningly premature. Religion, allied to nationalism, has emerged as perhaps the most powerful political force in the post cold-war world. Even in Britain, I suspect that we will hear more about it in the future than for a long time past. There will be the Decade of Evangelism; anguished voices within Islam; periodic tensions in Catholicism and perhaps the Jewish community as well. Religion will not seem merely marginal. It will be the arena of deep moral and social debates. In part this may be prompted by thoughts of the coming millennium. But in part it will reflect a growing realisation that we stand at a significant juncture of our cultural history, no less fateful than the one, two centuries ago, that brought forth the Enlightenment, the modern economy and the secular state.

We have run up against the limits of a certain view of human society: one that believed that progress was open-ended, that there was no limit to economic growth, that conflict always had a political solution, and that all solutions lay with either the individual or the state. We will search, as we have already begun to do, for an ethical vocabulary of duties as well as rights; for a new language of environmental restraint; for communities of shared responsibility and support; for relationships more enduring than those of temporary compatibility; and for that sense, that lies at the heart of the religious experience, that human life has meaning beyond the self.

These are themes central to the great religious traditions, and we will not have to re-invent them. I have suggested that, in a sense, we are already more religious than we assume. When we look at figures of church membership or attendance, ours seems to be a lapsed society. But there are more ways than this that religion enters our lives. The overwhelming majority of Britons still claim affiliation with the religion of their birth. An established Church places faith at the centre of our national symbols. We turn to worship at great moments of crisis or transition. Religion tells us who we are.

But more than that. If someone invented a religion detector and passed it over the surface of our culture, the needle would swing when he came to our still strong convictions that compassion and justice should be part of social order, that human life is sacred, that marriage and the nurture of children are not just one lifestyle among many. When we lack power, we still feel responsible. When we see others suffering, we can still feel pain. These are traces that the biblical tradition has left deep within our culture: signals of transcendence[7] that can at times move us to otherwise unaccountable acts of conscience and courage.

THE RENEWAL OF FAITH

However tenuous our religious attachments are, they have not yet ceased, and that means that they can be renewed. The question is, what form they will take. For the past century religion has been embattled and defensive. This has led to the two religious stances most common in the modern world, a diffuse liberalism on the one hand, sanctifying secular trends after the event; and a reactive extremism on the other, willing us back into a golden age that neither was nor will be again. The two live by their sibling rivalries, each seeing the other as the main threat to salvation. And they remind us that as well as being cohesive, religion can be divisive as well.

Neither, I believe, is the shape of a coherent future. Liberalism, by placing its faith in the individual, only accelerates the loss of community. Religious extremism, for its part, seeks to impose a single truth on a plural world. Together they suggest to an age already educated into scepticism that religion divides into the relevant but empty and the authentic but fanatical. These are not the religious imperatives of our time.

Religions are the structures of our common life. In their symbols and ceremonies, the lonely self finds communion with others who share a past and future and a commitment to both. In their visions, we discover the worth of un-self-interested action, and find, in the haunting words of the Rabbi of Kotzk, that God exists wherever we let Him in. Education and inspiration will renew our communities of faith. The question will be whether they can be revived without the intolerances that once made religion a source of prejudice as well as pride. In our plural, dangerous, interconnected world we can no longer afford to see God's image only in those who are in our image. It will take courageous leadership to remind us that after Babel, to be authentic to one truth does not mean being exclusive of others. A community of communities needs two kinds of religious strength: one to preserve our own distinct traditions, the other to bring them to an enlarged sense of the common good.

Faith persists and in persisting allows us to build a world more human than one in which men, nations or economic systems have become gods. Twenty years ago it seemed as if religion had run its course in the modern world. Today a more considered view would be that its story has hardly yet begun.

NOTES

1 Bryan Wilson, *Contemporary Transformations of Religion*, Oxford: Clarendon Press, 1979, 116.

2 Nathan Glazer, *American Judaism*, Chicago: University of Chicago Press, 1957.

3 Peter Berger, *The Sacred Canopy*, New York: Doubleday, 1967.

4 Robert Bellah, Richard Madsen, William Sullivan, Ann Swidler and Steven Tipton, *Habits of the Heart*, London, Hutchinson, 1988, 284.

5 See Martin Marty, *The Public Church*, New York: Crossroad, 1981, and *By Way of Response*, Nashville: Abingdon, 1981.

6 Quoted in Roger Scruton, *The Philosopher on Dover Beach*, London: Carcanet, 1990, 146.

7 The phrase is taken from Peter Berger, *A Rumour of Angels*, London: Allen Lane, 1970, 70.

7

AFTERWORD

There will be, predictably, objections to the concerns I have raised and the arguments I have advanced.

The first, surely, will be that the analysis is simply overoptimistic. Religion is not, in societies like Britain, the live force I have claimed it to be. Ted Honderich, for example, writing recently on Conservatism, dismisses religion as a factor in British life in two brisk sentences. 'The Church of England may once have been, but certainly is no longer, the Tory Party at prayer. There are not enough persons at prayer to make the idea compelling.'[1] Certainly such evidence as we have presents an overwhelming picture of declining church membership and attendance, a slow but continuing attrition within the mainstream denominations, and the progressive diminution of religious influence on personal and governmental decisions. The Jewish community, for its part, is not exempt from these trends; nor, I suspect, are other non-Christian faiths.

Perhaps so. But my argument is couched in broader terms than party politics, church attendance and the immediate future. Great harm is done to our understanding of religion by focusing only on its most visible effects and manifestations. The picture that thus emerges is of an overpoliticised religious leadership, vainly trying to compensate for unbelieving bishops, empty places of worship and internal dissension by pursuing an illusory influence on government policy. This caricature – the product of media fascination with conflict and confrontation – is a massive distortion. The most important religious dimensions of a culture are often those which are precisely not news.

I have suggested that such enduring commitments as we have to institutions like morality and the family are, ultimately, religious in character. The intellectual environment we inhabit, a heritage of that revolution in human consciousness called the Enlightenment, has systematically concealed that fact from us. We have assumed that such institutions could survive without a religious foundation – without, that is to say, the support of tradition, authority and community. I believe that to be a profound mistake, and one whose human consequences become ever more apparent.

It is not my argument that our religious traditions are in a state of good health. To the contrary: a situation in which a society is divided into a majority for whom religious ties are increasingly tenuous and a minority for whom they are sharply counter-cultural is one in which religion has lost its common, cohesive, collective character. It has ceased to be part of our moral environment, the air we breathe. At such a time, religions themselves splinter into liberals and neo-traditionalists who find that they have ever fewer values in common. Such has been the experience of all religions that have undergone the transformations of modernity. Religion then becomes not an alternative to, but itself a part of, the process of cultural fragmentation. There ceases to be a single Anglican or Catholic or Muslim or Jewish voice, or even a coherent conversation from which, ultimately, such a voice might emerge.

That is what I mean by speaking of a crisis in our moral ecology. But just as I believe that awareness of the crisis in our physical ecology will eventually bring about new restraints in our ethic of consumption, so I believe that awareness of a parallel crisis in our social and moral bonds will eventually produce new restraints in our ethic of individualism. We have consumed our religious resources without renewing them: therein lies the danger. They still persist and can be renewed: therein lies the hope.

I am neither an optimist nor a pessimist about the future of religion. George Steiner once made an important distinction between a prediction and a prophecy. A prediction which comes true is a success. A prophecy which comes true is a failure.[2] The prophet speaks of a possible future in order to arouse the hearts and minds of human beings to avert it. He does so because he believes that there is no inevitability in history. The future is made by the free choices of free moral agents. My argument is that continued secularisation will further fragment the institutions, traditions and loyalties which alone make social existence tolerable and humane. This will in turn provoke more extreme and intransigent religious reactions. That is a future I describe in order to avert, because I believe that it can be avoided.

It will be said, nonetheless, that we have already become too sceptical, unchurched and deracinated for religion to be renewed. Secularisation is a non-reversible process. Faith, once lost, cannot be recovered. Trying to reconstruct a broken tradition, as Wittgenstein once said, is like trying to mend a spider's web with human hands. The argument is plausible but, I think, untrue. We have not lost faith. As I point out in the lectures, surveys of religious opinion even in an unchurched society like Britain regularly reveal that something like nine out of ten of those questioned declare themselves to be Christians. The vast majority confess to a belief in God. Ours is not a nonbelieving society but a non-practising society. We have faith, but we tend not to observe its public rituals. Were religion indeed to have become meaningless in the minds of most people, doubts as to its future viability would indeed be justified. But that is not the case. If faith persists, then the values, institutions and communities associated with it can be recovered.

The renewal of our communities of faith is, necessarily, a responsibility not of governments but of religious institutions themselves. It is possible, nonetheless, to envisage policies that would, directly or indirectly, weaken those institutions, and to them I am personally opposed. They might include disestablishment of the Church of England, the abolition of the law on blasphemy, liberalisation of the law in relation to Sunday trading, opposition to denominational schools, and the dilution or marginalisation of religious education. Each of these would have the effect of signalling a further dissociation between religion and public culture, and would intensify the dangers of a collapse in our moral ecology.

It might seem paradoxical that one who speaks from within the Jewish tradition should seek to support institutions that are intrinsically Christian. But there is no paradox. Our particular faith is strengthened by the different particular faiths of others. And each of the many faiths that constitute a culturally plural Britain is diminished by a weakening of the faith of the majority. Religious traditions, though they have in the past often been mutually antagonistic, are in principle mutually supportive. Pluralism does not require the secularisation of public culture. Instead it calls for the cultivation of tolerance as a religious virtue.

RELIGION AND SOCIETY

The second objection, I suspect, will be to my understanding of what religion is. Why, in a series of lectures about religion, speak about morality, the family and pluralism rather than about faith, worship and salvation? Edward Norman put the point sharply in his 1978 Reith Lectures: 'Both in daily life and in the worship of the Church, the prevailing emphasis on the transformation of the material world has robbed men of their bridge to eternity.'[3] Surely religion is about the soul, not about society.

Here the Jewish perspective underlying the lectures is apparent. Judaism sees the transformation of the material world as the primary religious imperative. It is in our acts, relationships and social structures that we create holiness. The covenantal task is, in the words of a Jewish mystical tradition, 'to create a home for the Holy One, blessed be He, in the lower [physical] world.' Jewish law is concerned not only with penitence and prayer but with eating and drinking, sex and marriage, producing and trading, contracts and labour relations, the economy and the limits of government. If God is present everywhere, then every activity is sanctifiable. There are absolute commands and prohibitions. But there is no domain that is intrinsically and irredeemably secular. What is secular, said Rabbi Abraham HaKohen Kook, is what is *not yet holy*.

This tradition, deriving from the Mosaic and prophetic books and articulated in rabbinic law, has significant echoes in Christianity and Islam as well. To be sure, there are strands within Jewish mysticism and philosophy which emphasise contemplation and rapture, the silent encounter with the Infinite in the privacy of the soul. But for the most part, the lonely individual in communion with God is not the locus of Jewish spirituality. Instead Judaism finds religious meaning in the coming together of human beings in the presence of God and in obedience to His will. Judaism, as Yeshayahu Leibowitz pointed out,[4] is primarily concerned with the prose rather than the poetry of life, with the everyday rather than with the exceptional. *Halakhah*, Jewish law, is essentially a code for the sanctification of ordinary human acts and relations, and it always drew the Jewish contemplative back into engagement with the world.

To take one example: Moses Maimonides' *Guide for the Perplexed* [c. 1190], the greatest work of medieval Jewish philosophy, is an extreme statement of asceticism and intellectual meditation, explicitly written for a spiritual elite. Nonetheless, in the book's closing chapter, Maimonides writes that, having reached the heights of the knowledge of God, the believer must return to the struggles of society. Only then can he not merely *know* God, but also *imitate* Him. His prooftext is taken from Jeremiah 9:23, 'Let him who glories, glory in this: that he understands and knows Me, that I am the Lord who exercises kindness, justice and righteousness on earth, for in these I delight.' God is known not in His essence but in His deeds. Therefore true knowledge of God always leads back to society and to the creation of an environment of compassion and justice.

There are, admittedly, other conceptions of the religious domain. There are theologies which see religion as, in Plotinus' phrase, 'the flight of the alone to the Alone' and which teach disengagement from, and even despair of, the empirical world. I felt justified, however, in speaking from the biblical and rabbinic tradition not merely because it is my own, but because it challenges one of the great secularising forces of modernity: the idea that religion is a phenomenon of private life only. Religion and society are, on this account, two separate domains. I believe this to be a powerful but untenable idea. It results in what Richard Neuhaus calls 'the naked public square': a conception of society as secular and value-free, an arena in which all meanings and choices are essentially private. It should be apparent throughout these lectures that I regard this as a description not of an ideal society but of one close to disintegration. Such, I believe, is our situation and our danger.

The view that religion is essentially social must be distinguished from others with which it might be confused. I do not, for example, believe that great religious traditions can be reduced to political programmes, conservative or revolutionary. That error results from a failure to make the necessary distinctions between community and society, society and state, and state and government. Nor do I believe that religions are to be seen, as Durkheim saw them, as mere instruments of social cohesion. That view results in what Robert Bellah and others have described as 'civil religion,' the sacred endorsement of secular values. The difference between civil and traditional religion can be put bluntly: for the former God exists to serve society, for the latter, society exists to serve God. I do not believe that religion can be reduced to the canonisation of the status quo. Religious values are transcendent, not immanent; absolute, not relative. That means, necessarily, that there are times when religious leaders are called on to criticise prevailing ethical norms. Few things are more calculated to bring religion into disrepute than its futile pursuit of shifting moral fashion in the name of a 'revolutionary' theology, which is frequently neither revolutionary nor even, genuinely, theology.

I believe, quite simply, that the task of religious institutions is less to influence governments than to create communities of faith. When it comes to the family, for example, churches, synagogues and mosques are capable of exercising leadership, less by advocating specific programmes of legislation and taxation, than by the teaching and examples projected by religious schools and congregations. That is not to say that religious groups do not have an important contribution to make to political debate. They do. But to see this as the primary intersection between religion and society is, in my view, to make a twofold error. Firstly, it concedes to governments an omnipotence over social trends that they do not have. Secondly, it reduces morality to a matter of legislative constraints and financial inducements, thus preserving but secularising an old failure of religious ethics, namely seeing the moral life as a matter of punishments and rewards. Against this, I believe that social change begins in small communities like the family and the congregation, Burke's 'little platoons' or Berger's 'mediating structures'; and that morality is taught, not enforced. By becoming overpoliticised, religions risk forfeiting the influence they have for one that they cannot and should not have. Religions are less about changing government policies than about changing lives.

No less important, and frequently forgotten, is that religions are more embracing in the environments they create than what is narrowly termed 'political.' Consider, for example, the concept of equality. Rabbinic Judaism is, as I have pointed out elsewhere,[5] an egalitarian religion. But not in the economic sense normally attached to the term. There is, in the rabbinic tradition, a large literature devoted to the responsibilities of wealth and the alleviation of poverty. But there is no advocacy of state intervention to equalise incomes. The reason is simple. For the rabbis, economic goods are not the only, or even the most important, things of value. Instead there is the equality of rest guaranteed by the Sabbath, a day on which all hierarchies of power are suspended and the servant is as free as his master. There is the equality of access to knowledge, provided by the system of universal education initiated by Joshua ben Gamla in the Second Temple period,[6] and maintained by Jewish communities ever since. There is the equality of spiritual status, subsequent to the collapse of the institutions of priesthood and prophecy, which means that within rabbinic Judaism there is no elite of holy men with privileged esoteric wisdom and no class of persons with special ritual or salvific powers.

The idea of distributive justice depends, for its implications, not only on what counts as a just distribution, but on what things a culture values and therefore wishes to see equally distributed.[7] When religions become politicised there is a grave danger of seeing all values, directly or indirectly, as economic ones. One of the traditional tasks of religion was to remind us that this is not so. This is not to say that religions must be socially or economically conservative and that they are bound to endorse existing hierarchies of power. Against this, the entire thrust of the prophetic and rabbinic traditions is an eloquent refutation. But there are other and more significant ways in which a society can be unjust because unequal than can be measured by economic indicators. One of the dangers of religion in the middle ages was the risk of forgetting that man has a body. One of the dangers of religion today is the risk of forgetting that he has a soul.

So, to claim as I do that religions are the structures of our common life is not to argue for the politicisation or secularisation of religion, but on the contrary for the spiritualisation of society. Our public debates have taken place within an ever-diminishing conception of what matters, until we are left with only what can be quantified or legislated. All else, we have assumed, is private and intrinsically personal. Seldom can so impoverished a view have been taken of the public domain of our shared life and culture, and these lectures are an argument against it.

SOLUTION OR PROBLEM?

The final objection, and it is a powerful one, will come from those who will say that religion is not the solution to the dilemmas I have posed, but is instead part of the problem. The case can be made in either of two directions, depending on whether religious liberalism or extremism is our primary concern. Thus, I have argued for a strong defence of the stable nuclear family. But there are some voices within liberal Christianity and Judaism that would question the traditional sexual ethics on which the family is based. I have argued for the concept of moral authority. But there are liberal theologies which enthrone, at the heart of their systems, its opposite: moral autonomy. Religious liberalism, then, itself only serves to accelerate the breakdown of traditions which, I have suggested, is the devastating heritage of the Enlightenment.

In the opposite direction, I have argued for religious tolerance. But for some deeply religious individuals, integrity consists precisely in holy intransigence. I have argued that a plural society requires the maintenance of a national culture and the willingness of minority groups to come to terms with it. But that is precisely what religious purists would refuse to do. I have argued for a recovery of the sense of community: those structures of kinship and covenant larger than the individual but smaller than the state. But, as Roger Scruton reminds us, 'the real price of community' is 'sanctity, intolerance, exclusion, and a sense that life's meaning depends upon obedience, and also on vigilance against the enemy.'[8] There is, in short, no true community that is tolerant of outsiders. Religious extremism, then, accentuates rather than alleviates some of the conflicts I have diagnosed.

The objection, I believe, is well founded as far as it goes. Indeed, one of the essential themes of the lectures is to illustrate the ways in which religions become polarised by secularisation into liberal and extremist forms. Communities of faith do not stand outside the waves and currents of social forces but are themselves caught up in them. They can go with the flow of secular values or they can oppose the entire basis of plural democracies. In either case, they are of their time, and they take on its character. One of the hardest of all exercises of religious discernment is to judge whether a given social change represents spiritual growth or decline, and whether therefore it should be endorsed or fought. That is why I respect both liberal and extremist religious stances. But I cannot agree with either of them.

Liberal theologies, by conceding too much to passing moral fashion, have lost that sense of timelessness and transcendence which I believe to lie at the heart of the religious experience. They have had to shift their ground too often to give credence to claims to moral authority. They have sometimes been drawn in to unwise political allegiances, as if one could identify the Divine presence with a particular class or set of interests. They have emphasised the individual at the cost of community and the idea of choice at the expense of the command, and have thus contributed to the collapse of traditions and institutions – among them, the family – on which human flourishing depends. Above all, they have tended to make man the measure of God and reduce Divine imperatives to human needs.

Religious extremists, for their part, are often guilty of highly selective religious fervour. They respond to some religious texts but not to others. They attend to only an edited edition of religious doctrine. Standing as I do within a tradition that celebrated freedom, I cannot believe in the religious value of legislative coercion. Nor, as heir to the rabbinic heritage, can I believe that the worship of God demands the suppression of God's greatest creation, the human mind. Most emphatically, I cannot read the majestic opening chapters of the book of Genesis, with their insistence on the sanctity of human life as such, without wondering how faith can lead human beings to deny rights to others on the grounds of faith. That has been the history of most religious groups at most times when they held political power. But it remains a scandal and a desecration, and one whose price in this century of mass destruction has become finally too high. The subordination of religion to human interests and animosities is, in the last analysis, idolatry.

I cannot hide my fears that the future, even as it discloses possibilities of religious renewal, contains a great danger of regression into religious hostilities. The recent history of Protestants and Catholics in Northern Ireland, Muslims and Christians in Lebanon, Muslims and Hindus in India, Jews and Muslims in the Middle East and the emergent religious rivalries in the Soviet Union do not bode well. Even in Britain and America, ethnic conflict is often heightened by religious or quasi-religious motifs.

The argument of my fifth lecture is that the problem of religious intolerance has not yet been adequately addressed. The assumption of the Enlightenment was that it would be solved in the simplest way possible. Intolerance would disappear because religion would disappear. The refutation was not long in coming. On 26 August 1789, the revolutionary French National Assembly issued its declaration of the Rights of Man, including the statement that 'No person shall be molested for his opinions, even such as are religious.' Immediately thereafter, there were savage riots in Alsace against the Jews. A century later, as antisemitism gathered momentum throughout Europe, it had become clear that religious prejudice had far greater powers of survival than religious faith.

To be sure, in the aftermath of the Holocaust, a worldwide movement began toward inter-religious dialogue. It was born of the by then necessary conviction that faiths must talk together if they are to live together. The movement has had achievements. The Vatican declaration *Nostra Aetate*, in 1965, was one. The 1988 Lambeth resolution on 'The Way of Dialogue' was another. Perhaps, given the sheer weight of persisting prejudice, these were great achievements. But they were beset by reservations and qualifications. What they said was less significant than what they did not say. The problem lies not so much at those exalted altitudes where individuals of great breadth of vision meet and find, as Martin Buber would have put it, God in meeting. It lies nearer to the base of the mountain, where faith still resides in exclusion. The writings of Rosemary Radford Reuther and John Hick, for example, have given us a glimpse of how revolutionary the change would have to be in Christian theology if the equal integrity of other faiths is to be affirmed. Within Islam the process of reflection on religious pluralism has not yet reached even this stage.

The objection, then, is valid if the only religious alternatives available in a secular age are theological liberalism and extremism. But I believe that these are not the only alternatives. More than that: I believe that neither is fully sensitive to the commanding voice of faith. The religious imperative at any age is born at the intersection of the timeless and the time-bound. We must not lose our ability to hear, across the generations, the transcendent voice of revelation: that is the argument against liberalism. But neither may we apply the texts of revelation as if nothing significant had changed in the human situation in the intervening years: that is the argument against extremism. Liberalism grants too much to the present, extremism too much to the past. Against both, the task of the sage, prophet or religious philosopher has always been to mediate between the two, between ancient texts and present contexts, the former determining our aspirations, the latter, their field of application. Religious moderation – the ability to interpret past ideals in terms of present possibilities – is not, as it is so often thought to be nowadays, a failure of integrity or authenticity. It is, quite simply, high religious art.

Conventional opinion notwithstanding, I am convinced that religions can be both faithful to their traditions and answerable to the imperative of tolerance. They can come to terms with other cultures without sacrificing their identity.

They can be responsive to social change without at the same time assenting to every ephemeral shift in moral mood. Not only do I believe this to be possible, I believe it to be necessary. Religious liberalism has already taken us too far down the rapids of institutional and moral collapse. Religious extremism has brought us repeatedly to war and bloodshed. How many more lives must be lost before we are forced to the conclusion that God has created many faiths but only one world in which to live? The rabbis said that one who destroys a human life is as if he had destroyed a universe. In the late twentieth century the 'as if' is terribly close. The destruction of the universe has become not metaphor but possibility.

I believe that our capacity to recognise the 'wholly Other' that is God is measured by our ability to recognise the image of God that resides in the person who is not like us: the human 'wholly other.' The Bible commands us only once to love our neighbour. But it never tires of urging us to love the stranger. To have faith in God as creator and ruler of the universe is to do more than to believe that God has spoken to us. It is to believe that God has spoken to others, in a language which we may not understand. After Babel, there is no one universal language which alone comprehends God, such that those who do not speak it are excluded from salvation, redemption or truth. Until that proposition frames our religious imagination, our faiths will contain devastating possibilities.

Religion, then, *is* part of the problem. But it is also and necessarily part of the solution. The recovery of the values and institutions necessary to our moral ecology cannot take place without the reinstatement of their foundations, which are ultimately religious. The alternatives have been tried these past two centuries, and have been found wanting. Neither the individual nor the state – the two key entities of a secular order – is an adequate base of a moral society. Two centuries after the French revolution, we stand on the brink of another momentous turn in our intellectual orientation. Increasingly as we approach the millennium we will begin to see that the battle of the human future will not be fought against religion or independently of it, but *within* the great religions themselves. Can they re-establish their cogency and persuasive power? And can they do so without resurrecting the antagonisms and intolerances of the past? These will be the questions on which much else will turn.

I believe that religions do not need to be authoritarian to possess authority, nor need they be exclusive to be authentic. Their influence lies only in the force of their example, the cogency of their teachings and the spiritual beauty of the lives they inspire. They must maintain a critical distance from the values of the age, speaking if necessary against even those social trends that seem to be inevitable, knowing as they do that there is no inevitability in human affairs and that a choice between good and evil is always before us. But that distance must not be so great as to condemn in advance the changes that are a necessary part of the development of civilisation, for God asks us to live in our time, not in any other, neither an imagined past nor a utopian future.

In the beginning, God created the world. Thereafter He entrusted us to create a human world which will be, in the structures of our common life, a home for the Divine presence. That command still addresses us with its momentous challenge, the persisting call of faith.

NOTES

1 Ted Honderich, *Conservatism*, London: Hamish Hamilton, 1990, 168.
2 This, of course, is the theme of the biblical book of Jonah.
3 Edward Norman, *Christianity and the World Order*, BBC, 1978, lecture 6.

4   Yeshayahu Leibowitz [b. 1903] is a leading, though consistently controversial, Israeli Orthodox thinker. Most of his works are untranslated into English, but his view of Judaism is summarised in his article, 'Commandments,' in Arthur A. Cohen and Paul Mendes-Flohr (eds.), *Contemporary Jewish Religious- Thought*, New York: Charles Scribner's, 67–80

5   See, for example, Jonathan Sacks, *Tradition in an Untraditional Age*, London: Vallentine, Mitchell, 1990, 183–202.

6   Babylonian Talmud, *Baba Batra* 21a.

7   This point is well made in Michael Walzer, *Spheres of Justice*, Oxford: Blackwell, 1983.

8   Roger Scruton, *The Philosopher on Dover Beach*, London: Carcanet, 1990, 310.

FURTHER READING

1 THE ENVIRONMENT OF FAITH

On secularisation and modernity, I have been influenced by the sociology of knowledge approach of Peter L. Berger. See his *The Sacred Canopy*, New York: Doubleday, 1967; *Facing Up to Modernity*, London: Penguin, 1979; *Invitation to Sociology*, London: Penguin, 1966; Peter L. Berger and Thomas Luckman, *The Social Construction of Reality*, London: Penguin, 1971; Peter L. Berger, Brigitte Berger and Hansfried Kellner, *The Homeless Mind*, London: Penguin, 1973; and Peter L. Berger and Hansfried Kellner, *Sociology Reinterpreted*, London: Pelican, 1982. Berger's own attempts to address religiously the questions he raises as a sociologist are contained in his *A Rumour of Angels*, London: Allen Lane, 1970, and *The Heretical Imperative*, New York: Doubleday, 1979. Berger's work is discussed in James Davison Hunter and Stephen C. Ainlay (eds.), *Making Sense of Modern Times: Peter L. Berger and the Vision of Interpretive Sociology*, London: Routledge and Kegan Paul, 1986.

On secularisation, see also Bryan Wilson, *Religion in a Secular Society*, London: Pelican 1969; *Contemporary Transformations of Religion*, Oxford: Oxford University Press, 1976; *Religion in Sociological Perspective*, Oxford: Oxford University Press, 1982; Michael Hill, *A Sociology of Religion*, London: Heinemann, 1973; David Martin, *The Religious and the Secular*, New York: Schocken Books. 1969; David Martin, *A General Theory of Secularisation*, Oxford: Basil Blackwell, 1978; and Charles Y. Glock and Rodney Stark, *Religion and Society in Tension*, Chicago: Rand McNally, 1965.

Useful studies of the intellectual history of secularisation are Owen Chadwick, *The Secularisation of the European Mind in the Nineteenth Century*, Cambridge: Cambridge University Press, 1975; and Don Cupitt, *The Sea of Faith,* London: BBC, 1985.

On the secularisation of contemporary British society, see Alan D. Gilbert, *The Making of Post-Christian Britain*, London: Longman, 1980; and Kenneth Medhurst and George Moyser, *Church and Politics in a Secular Age*, Oxford: Clarendon Press, 1988; Terence Thomas (ed.), *The British: Their Religious Beliefs and Practices 1800–1986*, London: Routledge, 1988. Christian responses to the dilemmas of secularisation are contained in John Habgood, *Church and Nation in a Secular Age*, London: Darton Longman and Todd, 1983; and the General Synod's Board for Social Responsibility, *Changing Britain: Social Diversity and Moral Unity*, London: Church House Publishing, 1987.

The persisting strength of religion, especially in America, has resulted in important reconsiderations of the secularisation thesis. See, in particular, Daniel Bell, 'Return of the Sacred? The Argument on the Future of Religion,' *British Journal of Sociology* 38 (December 1977): 419–449; Phillip E. Hammond, *The Sacred in a Secular Age*, Berkeley: University of California Press, 1985; Martin Marty, 'Religion in America since Mid- Century.' *Daedalus* 111: 149–163; John Neuhaus (ed.), *Unsecular America*, Grand Rapids, Michigan: William Eerdmans, 1986. Also of interest in this context are Charles Glock and Robert Bellah (eds.). *The New Religious Consciousness*, Berkeley: University of California Press, 1976 and Andrew Greeley, *Unsecular Man*, New York: Schocken Books, 1975.

2 DEMORALISATION

My starting point for this chapter was the much discussed work of Alasdair MacIntyre, *After Virtue*, London: Duckworth, 1981. The argument is taken further in his *Whose Justice? Which Rationality?*,

London: Duckworth, 1988, and *Three Rival Versions of Moral Enquiry*, London: Duckworth, 1990. Also of interest are his earlier works, *A Short History of Ethics*, London: Routledge and Kegan Paul, 1967, *Against the Self-Images of the Age*, London: Duckworth, 1971, and especially *Secularization and Moral Change*, London: Oxford University Press, 1967. MacIntyre's ideas are developed in a theological context in Stanley Hauerwas, *The Peaceable Kingdom*, London: SCM, 1983.

Other thinkers have addressed the broad issues of the relationship between ethics, narrative, tradition and community, and have raised questions about the concept of self divorced from constitutive attachments. See especially, Stuart Hampshire, *Morality and Conflict*, Oxford: Blackwell, 1983; Michael Sandel, *Liberalism and the Limits of Justice*, Cambridge: Cambridge University Press, 1982; Michael Sandel (ed.), *Liberalism and its Critics*, Oxford: Blackwell, 1984; Michael Walzer, *Spheres of Justice*, Oxford: Blackwell, 1983; Richard J. Bernstein, *Beyond Objectivism and Relativism*, Oxford: Blackwell, 1983; Jeffrey Stout, *Ethics After Babel* Boston: Beacon Press, 1988; Charles Taylor, *Hegel and Modern Society*, Cambridge: Cambridge University Press, 1979, and the same author's *Philosophy and the Human Sciences*, Cambridge: Cambridge University Press, 1985, and *Sources of the Self* Cambridge: Cambridge University Press, 1989.

Particularly valuable for an understanding of the history of the self is Lionel Trilling's *Sincerity and Authenticity*, Cambridge, Mass.: Harvard University Press, 1978. Other important works which have a direct bearing on the themes of this chapter include Hans-Georg Gadamer, *Truth and Method*, New York: Crossroad, 1985; E. H. Gombrich, *Art and Illusion*, Oxford: Phaidon, 1960; Edward Shils, *Tradition*, London: Faber and Faber, 1981; and Jaroslav Pelikan, *The Vindication of Tradition*, New Haven: Yale University Press, 1984.

The classic discussion of the relation between law and morals is contained in Patrick Devlin, *The Enforcement of Morals*,

Oxford: Oxford University Press, 1968 and H. L. A. Hart, *Law, Liberty and Morality*, Oxford: Oxford University Press, 1968. For a more recent discussion, see Simon Lee, *Law and Morals*, Oxford: Oxford University Press, 1986. See also Ronald Dworkin, *Law's Empire*, London: Fontana, 1986 and *A Matter of Principle,* Oxford: Clarendon Press, 1986.

For direct exploration of the theme of religion and ethics, see Paul Helm (ed.), *Divine Commands and Morality*, Oxford: Oxford University Press, 1981; Don Cupitt, *Crisis of Moral Authority*, London: SCM, 1972; Peter Geach, *God and the Soul*, London: Routledge and Kegan Paul, 1978; and Basil Mitchell, *Morality: Religious and Secular*, Oxford: Clarendon Press, 1980.

3 THE FRAGILE FAMILY

Useful discussions of the family are contained in Digby Anderson and Graham Dawson (eds.), *Family Portraits*, London: Social Affairs Unit, 1986; Brigitte Berger and Peter Berger, *The War over the Family*, Harmondsworth: Penguin, 1984; Ronald Fletcher, *The Shaking of the Foundations: Family and Society*, London: Routledge, 1988; Christopher Lasch: *Haven in a Heartless World*, New York: Basic Books, 1977; Ferdinand Mount, *The Subversive Family*, London: Jonathan Cape, 1970; R. N. Rapoport, M. P. Fogarty and R. Rapoport (eds.), *Families in Britain*, London: Routledge, 1982; Valerie Polakow Suransky, *The Erosion of Childhood*, Chicago: University of Chicago Press, 1982. Emmanuel Todd's *The Explanation of Ideology*, Oxford: Blackwell, 1988, argues a close connection between family structure and political ideology.

For information on the current state of the family see Kathleen Kiernan and Malcolm Wicks, *Family Change and Future Policy*, London: Family Policy Centre, 1990; and Roger Jowell, Sharon Witherspoon and Lindsay Brook (eds.), *British Social Attitudes*, London: Gower, 1989, 143–156.

Aspects of Jewish teaching in relation to the family are explored in Gerald Blidstein, *Honour Thy Father and Mother*, New York: Ktav, 1975; Reuven Bulka, *Jewish Marriage: A Halakhic Ethic*, New York: Ktav, 1986; David Feldman, *Marital Relations, Birth Control and Abortion in Jewish Law*, New York: Schocken, 1974; David Kraemer (ed.), *The Jewish Family: Metaphor and Memory*, New York: Oxford University Press, 1989; and Maurice Lamm, *The Jewish Way in Love and Marriage*, San Francisco: Harper and Row, 1980. Christian teaching on these themes is presented by Jack Dominion, *Marriage, Faith and Love*, London: Fount Paperbacks, 1984; and *Sexual Integrity*, London: Darton, Longman and Todd, 1987.

On the concept of 'mediating structures' between the individual and the state, see Peter L. Berger and Richard John Neuhaus, *To Empower People*, Washington: American Enterprise Institute for Public Policy Research, 1977 and Peter Berger, 'In Praise of Particularity,' in his *Facing Up to Modernity*, 167–180. See also Charles Murray, 'In Pursuit of Happiness,' *Dialogue* 87 (1990), 41–47.

4 PARADOXES OF PLURALISM

Basil Mitchell's pamphlet, *Why Social Policy Cannot be Morally Neutral: The Current Confusion about Pluralism,* London: Social Affairs Unit, 1989, is an excellent introduction to the problems examined in this chapter, as is J. D. Green, 'Beyond the Satanic Verses,' *Encounter*, June 1990, 12–20. For different perspectives, see Joseph Raz, *The Morality of Freedom*, Oxford: Clarendon Press, 1988 and *Britain: A Plural Society*, London: Commission for Racial Equality, 1990.

On ethnicity, see Nathan Glazer and Daniel P. Moynihan, *Beyond the Melting Pot*, Cambridge, Mass.: MIT Press, 1970; Michael Novak, *The Rise of the Unmeltable Ethnics*, New York: Macmillan: 1972; and Joseph Rothschild, *Ethnopolitics: A*

Conceptual Framework, New York: Columbia University Press, 1981.

Blasphemy is considered in Leonard W. Levy, *Treason Against God*, New York: Schocken Books, 1981; Nicholas Walter, *Blasphemy, Ancient and Modern*, London: Rationalist Press Association, 1990; Richard Webster, *A Brief History of Blasphemy*, Suffolk: The Orwell Press, 1990; F. LaGard Smith, *Blasphemy and the Battle for Faith*, London: Hodder and Stoughton, 1990; *Law, Blasphemy and the Multi-Faith Society*, London: Commission for Racial Equality, 1990 and *Free Speech*, London: Commission for Racial Equality, 1990. Specifically on the Rushdie affair, see Lisa Appignanesi and Sara Maitland, *The Rushdie File*, London: Fourth Estate, 1989; Fay Weldon, *Sacred Cows*, London: Chatto and Windus, 1989 and Malise Ruthven, *A Satanic Affair*, London: Chatto and Windus, 1990.

On denominational schooling, see Mervyn Hiskett, *Schooling for British Muslims*, London: The Social Affairs Unit, 1989 and *Schools of Faith*, London: Commission for Racial Equality, 1990.

5 FUNDAMENTALISM

On the rise of conservative Christianity in America, see Dean Kelley, *Why Conservative Churches are Growing*, New York: Harper and Row, 1972; the same author's 'Why Conservative Churches are still Growing,' *Journal for the Scientific Study of Religion* 17, 165–172; and Reginald Bibby, 'Why Conservative Churches *Really* Are Growing: Kelley Revisited,' *Journal for the Scientific Study of Religion* 17, 129–137. On the parallel rise of Orthodox Judaism, see Reuven Bulka (ed.), *Dimensions of Orthodox Judaism*, New York: Ktav, 1983.

The history of evangelical Christianity in America is charted in James Davison Hunter's *American Evangelicalism: Conservative Religion and the Quandary of Modernity*, New Brunswick, N.J.: Rutgers University Press, 1983 and *Evangelicalism: The*

Coming Generation, Chicago: University of Chicago Press, 1987. On American fundamentalism, see E. Sandeen, *The Roots of Fundamentalism*, Chicago: University of Chicago Press, 1970 and George M. Marsden, *Fundamentalism and American Culture*, New York: Oxford University Press, 1980. The key documents of the early period of fundamentalism are reproduced in the 45 volume series, *Fundamentalism in American Religion 1880-1950*, edited by Joel E. Carpenter, New York: Garland.

The political influence of the movement in recent decades is explored in Erling Jorstad, *Evangelicals in the White House: The Cultural Maturation of Born Again Christianity 1960–1981*, New York and Toronto: Edwin Mellen Press, 1981 and Anson Shupe and William A. Stacey, *Born Again Politics and the Moral Majority*, New York and Toronto: Edwin Mellen Press, 1982. See also Ronald B. Flowers, *Religion in Strange Times*, Mercer University Press, 1984. Tele-evangelism is evaluated in Peter Elvy, *Buying Time*, Essex: McCrimmons, 1986 and Steven Bruce, *Pray TV*, London: Routledge, 1990. A useful anthology of recent expressions of and responses to American fundamentalism is Richard John Neuhaus and Michael Cromartie (eds.), *Piety and Politics: Evangelicals and Fundamentalists Confront the World*, Washington: Ethics and Public Policy Center, 1989.

James Barr's *Fundamentalism*, London: SCM, 1977, and *Escaping from Fundamentalism*, London: SCM, 1984, are strongly argued objections to a Christian fundamentalist reading of biblical texts. I defend an Orthodox Jewish approach to religious texts in 'Fundamentalism Reconsidered,' *L'Eylah: A Journal of Judaism Today* 28 (September 1989), 8–13. The worldwide rise of fundamentalism in different religious traditions is explored in Lionel Caplan (ed.), *Studies in Religious Fundamentalism*, London: Macmillan, 1987.

Within Judaism, discussion of fundamentalism is marred by a failure to distinguish at least three separate issues: the authority of rabbinic tradition, the relationship between Judaism and modern culture, and the application of religious texts to contemporary political questions. The first separates Orthodox Jews from others, the second and third represent different divisions within Orthodoxy. The theological and sociological dimensions of Orthodoxy's encounter with modernity are explored in Jonathan Sacks, *Traditional Alternatives*, London: Jews' College Publications, 1989 and *Tradition in an Untraditional Age*, London: Vallentine, Mitchell, 1990 and Jonathan Sacks (ed.), *Orthodoxy Confronts Modernity*, New York: Ktav, forthcoming.

For a spirited defence of an Orthodoxy open to modern culture, see Norman Lamm, *Torah Umadda: The Encounter of Religious Learning and Worldly Knowledge in the Jewish Tradition*, New York: Ktav, 1990. Secularist perspectives on the relationship between religion and state in contemporary Israel are presented in Amos Oz, *In the Land of Israel*, London: Flamingo, 1983; Amnon Rubinstein, *The Zionist Dream Revisited*, New York: Schocken, 1984; Yehoshafat Harkabi, *Israel's Fateful Decisions*, London: I. B. Tauris, 1988; and Gershon Weiler, *Jewish Theocracy*, Leiden: Brill, 1988. Religious perspectives are represented in Shubert Spero and Yitzchak Pessin (eds.) *Religious Zionism*, Jerusalem: World Zionist Organisation, 1989. Uriel Tal's essay, 'Contemporary Hermeneutics and Self-Views on the Relationship between State and Land,' in Lawrence A. Hoffman (ed.), *The Land of Israel*, Indiana: University of Notre Dame Press, 1986, 316–338, is an excellent analysis of the different ways in which Orthodox Jews in Israel interpret political issues in the light of tradition and sacred texts.

On Islam in the modern world, see Malise Ruthven, *Islam in the World*, Harmondsworth: Penguin, 1984; W. Montgomery Watt, *Islamic Fundamentalism and Modernity*, London: Routledge, 1988; Fazlur Rahman, *Islam and Modernity*, Chicago: University of Chicago Press, 1982; R. Hrair Dekmejian, *Islam in Revolution*, Syracuse: Syracuse University Press, 1985; David Pryce-Jones, *The Closed Circle*, London: Weidenfeld and Nicolson, 1989;

Akbar Ahmed, *Discovering Islam*, London: Routledge, 1988; Elie Kedourie, *Islam in the Modern World*, London: Mansell, 1980. An important text is Imam Khomeini, *Islam and Revolution*, translated by Hamid Algar, London: KPI, 1985. On Islamic fundamentalism and Judaism, see Ronald L. Nettler, *Past Trials and Present Tribulations*, Oxford: Pergamon, 1987.

The problems of religious conflict in contemporary America are explored in Robert Bellah and Frederick Greenspahn (eds.), *Uncivil Religion*, New York: Crossroad, 1987. Religious pluralism is discussed in John Hick, *Problems of Religious Pluralism*, London: Macmillan, 1985; Alastair Hunter, *Christianity and Other Faiths in Britain*, London: SCM, 1985; John Hick and Paul Knitter (eds.), *The Myth of Christian Uniqueness*, London: SCM, 1987; David Tracy, *Plurality and Ambiguity*, London: SCM, 1987.

6 A COMMUNITY OF COMMUNITIES

Recent studies of Anglo-Jewry at the end of the nineteenth century include Eugene C. Black, *The Social Politics of Anglo-Jewry 1880–1920*, Oxford: Blackwell, 1988; Vivian Lipman, *A History of the Jews in Britain since 1858*, Leicester University Press, 1990; and David Cesarani (ed.), *The Making of Modern Anglo-Jewry*, Oxford: Blackwell, 1990. Also of interest are Anne and Roger Cowen, *Victorian Jews through British Eyes*, Oxford: Littman Library/ Oxford University Press, 1987 and Bill Williams, *Manchester Jewry: A Pictorial History 1788–1988*, Manchester: Archive Publications, 1988. On the current state of diaspora Jewry, the literature is overwhelmingly focused on America. See Steven M. Cohen, *American Assimilation or Jewish Revival?*, Bloomington: Indiana University Press, 1988; Calvin Goldscheider, *Jewish Continuity and Change*, Bloomington: Indiana University Press, 1986; Charles Liebman, *Deceptive Images*, New Brunswick: Transaction Books, 1988; Nathan Glazer, *New Perspectives in American Jewish*

Sociology, New York: American Jewish Committee, 1987; and Charles E. Silberman, *A Certain People*, New York: Summit, 1985.

Relevant to the argument of this chapter, and to the lectures as a whole, are Alexis de Tocqueville, *Democracy in America*, translated by George Lawrence, London: Fontana, 1968; Max Weber, *The Protestant Ethic and the Spirit of Capitalism*, translated by Talcott Parsons, London: Unwin, 1987; Daniel Bell, *The Cultural Contradictions of Capitalism*, New York: Basic Books, 1976; Robert N. Bellah, *Beyond Belief*, New York: Harper and Row, 1970, and the same author's *The Broken Covenant: American Civil Religion in Time of Trial*, New York: Seabury Press, 1975; Robert Bellah, Richard Madsen, William M. Sullivan, Ann Swidler and Steven M. Tipton, *Habits of the Heart: Middle America Observed*, London: Hutchinson, 1988; Martin Marty, *The Public Churchy* New York: Crossroad, 1981, and *By Way of Response*, Nashville: Abingdon, 1981; Richard John Neuhaus, *The Naked Public Square*, Grand Rapids, Michigan: Eerdmans, 1984; Michael Novak, *The Spirit of Democratic Capitalism*, New York: Simon and Schuster, 1982 and *Morality, Capitalism and Democracy*, London: Institute of Economic Affairs, 1990.